FOURTH EDITION

Career Development

Strategies and Technologies for Career and Life Balance

MONICA E. BREIDENBACH

Prentice
Hall

Upper Saddle River, New Jersey 07458

Library of Congress Cataloging-in-Publication Data

Breidenbach, Monica E.
    Career development : strategies and technologies for career and life balance / Monica E.
Breidenbach.—4th ed.
        p.   cm.
    Includes bibliographical references and index.
    ISBN 0-13-086759-4
    1. Career development.   I. Title.

HF5549.5.C35 B74 2000+
650.14—dc21

00-062414

Acquisitions Editor: Sande Johnson
Assistant Editor: Michelle Williams
Production Editor: Holcomb Hathaway
Director of Manufacturing and Production: Bruce Johnson
Managing Editor: Mary Carnis
Manufacturing Manager: Ed O'Dougherty
Art Director: Marianne Frasco
Marketing Manager: Jeff McIlroy
Marketing Assistant: Barbara Rosenberg
Cover Design: Joe Sengotta
Cover Art: Jude Maceren, Images.com/SIS
Composition: Aerocraft Charter Art Service
Printing and Binding: The Banta Company

Prentice-Hall International (UK) Limited, *London*
Prentice-Hall of Australia Pty. Limited, *Sydney*
Prentice-Hall Canada Inc., *Toronto*
Prentice-Hall Hispanoamericana, S.A., *Mexico*
Prentice-Hall of India Private Limited, *New Delhi*
Prentice-Hall of Japan, Inc., *Tokyo*
Pearson Education Singapore Pte. Ltd.
Editora Prentice-Hall do Brasil, Ltda., *Rio de Janeiro*

10 9 8 7 6 5 4 3 2 1
ISBN 0-13-086759-4

Contents

Preface

Today's market is ripe for the well-prepared and focused job searcher. College graduates have more opportunities for better jobs where they can improve their status on the job as well as with continuing education.

What makes today's market a good market is twofold: The rise in the need for college graduates in almost every field and the improvement of technology, which continues to improve exponentially.

Time used to be when a job search was hard work. Only typewriters were available to provide letters and résumés in professional styles. Interview by interview was the only way to contact people to determine interest. Company profiles were hard to come by unless you knew someone inside an organization.

Job searching still is a difficult and time-consuming process. It requires full-time attention. However, the tools to assist with the search are more prevalent, easier to use, and the process is very professional, quick, and pervasive.

Do not be misled into thinking that job searching is a linear process today, anymore than it ever was. The process is a zigzag, back and forth effort on the part of the searcher. "Zigzagging" will happen if you implement the plan to see at least 40 people a week on a full-time search or limit yourself to a 20 people a week part-time search.

Example: research into "business profiles" will come into play:

a. when you are considering what companies may need your skills and talent;

b. when you look for Career Fairs to attend with your first (new) résumé;

c. when you identify management levels to consider your résumé;

d. when you consider just what kind of résumé posting firm you want to use;

e. when you decide where/when to store information for easy access when employers call;

f. and when they contact you by e-mail or some other electronic connection, you need to have your files in a ready access state.

"Career Fairs" is another research item that reoccurs:

a. when you are considering which one to attend;
b. when you identify your purpose for attending—knowledge, connections, new information, etc.;
c. when you compare professional opportunities in a broader context;
d. and when looking for new fields and jobs potential.

Your need for reference and research materials constantly zigzags back and forth throughout your campaign. So do not be alarmed if you notice reference to various components of the process show up again and again in the text.

What this is telling you is, "Format a clear and accurately named set of files." Examine the "why now?" in each case and you will notice a new focus for your use of the term. This will help expand your continuing breadth of information, job searching process, and counsel.

The subtitle of this book is *Strategies and Technologies for Career and Life Balance.* Twenty-four hours a day, seven days a week a job searcher must be visible in the marketplace in order to locate the choicest jobs possible given one's education, experience, skills, and talents.

The only way a searcher can be available at this scope and rate is with the use and extension the newest technologies provide. One must be computer and network literate or you will be left in the dust of your contemporaries.

This text emphasizes the need for constantly measuring career goals against life goals, and wherever possible combining the two to succeed in both. If you want a family, consider whether a traveling sales job/career may prohibit your participation a bit in your family's development. (See: Arthur Miller's *Death of a Salesman.*) If you want to travel then do it before you start a family.

You need the support of your family and friends throughout your life so dismissing them for some part of your life while you leap to new heights in a career without considering them may produce a friendless and lonely life in your after work activities. It is lonely at the top. Booze is effective in killing the pain, but the pain manages to find you again in the morning. (See: Eugene O'Neill's *A Long Day's Journey Into Night.*)

Themes of the Text

The cycle of job searching is endless and constant. The major themes are research, marketing focus, résumés, interviewing, negotiations, politics, and financial awareness. Once a job option is accepted, the search begins for the next opportunity. This requires sensitivity to your own continuing education goals, knowing if and when your own career goals may change, awareness of the industry's options/problems/growth, and the needs of the market.

These areas are addressed separately in different chapters and infused into many other chapters for the searcher to make the connecting links in understanding the job market and this search process. The goal is to find the choicest job in your respective field that you can handle successfully.

TOPIC	CONCENTRATION	INTEGRATION
Research	Chapter 1	All chapters
Résumés	Chapters 1, 2, and 3	Chapters 4, 7, 8, and 10
Interviewing	Chapters 4 and 5	Chapters 3, 6, and 10–13
Negotiations	Chapter 6	Chapters 11 through 14
Marketing	Chapters 7, 8, and 9	Chapters 2, 4, and 10
Politics	Chapter 10	Chapters 5, 6, 9, and 14
Financial Literacy	Chapters 11 through 14	Chapters 3, 4, 6, and 10

The market's needs are global, no matter your chosen field. Below is a short summary of the chapter contents for an overview.

Section One clearly explains the steps to follow when preparing your résumé. Chapter 1 directs the searcher to follow a clear outline or plan of operation to prepare for assembling résumé information that will enable a professional-looking representation of one's readiness for the market of choice, which will be obvious to those who receive this résumé.

Chapter 2 focuses on the variety of forms that a résumé is now accepted in the marketplace. If you are searching in international markets, the *curriculum vitae* is explained with advice about how to proceed in another country where the language is not English. New formats for business cards are revealed. Searching for company profiles to augment your decision about where to search is also developed in Chapter 2.

Chapter 3 covers cyberspace résumés, which are hot in today's market. Cool design and killer content are imperative to make a good first impression. Your résumé reaches the decision makers before you do. CD-ROM business cards are introduced as résumé substitutes, and sites where these are available are listed. How to approach and submit résumés to résumé posting services are also described.

Section Two describes different types of interviews and prepares you to negotiate for the best salary and benefits possible. Chapter 4 describes the subdivisions of Internet use and career fairs' potential for the job searcher. These interviews are basically informational interviews, but can lead to more substantive job interviews if worked for their potential effectiveness. Working existing networks and forming new ones are both part of this chapter.

Knowing how to answer an ad so that you are considered for the position is an art, and the rules can be learned by anyone, as explained in Chapter 5. Importance of company knowledge before the interview is stressed. Understand that "experiences" in an interview situation refer to people, challenges, problems, options, and resolutions that have been a part of your past. To most interviewers, the best predictor of your future success with them is your past success with other employers.

Chapter 6 introduces the GAME *theory* of John von Neumann and John Forbes Nash, Jr. I have translated and processed their theory to apply to negotiations, and the 3-step charted process is in this chapter. Understand the financial options that are available for the now (what comes out of your check) and the future (what you have saved for retirement). Creative and imaginative ways that employers are figuring out to reward employees go beyond salary. They are more numerous and inventive among today's managerial options.

In Section Three you will learn what it takes to put your best foot forward in today's job market. To understand that looking for a job is essentially a marketing process is difficult for some to grasp as explained in Chapter 7. If you work it, marketing is to the advantage of the searcher. You are the product, the salary range is the price, your résumé is the promotional ad, and the distribution is wherever you send the résumé given 24/7 options to deliver the good news that you are available for the market.

Market potential is described as unlimited and global in Chapter 8. Using e-commerce, there are constant changes and unpredictability about tools and methods for designing an effective search. A market plan and strategy need to be designed at the outset so you won't be overwhelmed and thus unable to take advantage of the opportunities that will come your way with these suggestions.

Chapter 9 introduces entrepreneurship. Entrepreneurship is for a few. Learning what a risk taker you are, what newness you may bring to the market, who will be there to assist you, and what success can you expect are all questions that need to be answered before you make this leap where only about 2 percent of the American populace ever goes. Knowing about Web page design and e-business techniques cannot be highlighted enough to prepare anyone for this leap of faith.

Chapter 10 delves into office politics: It is a big bear to some, an unavoidable menace to many, a mystery to a few, and an opportunity to the chosen. Defining terms, knowing a company's history as well as its culture, and understanding who has the power and wields it fairly or unfairly are all things one needs to know. You cannot avoid being in politics because you are in the business. So do your best to understand what is going on and learn how to cope most effectively for your own ends and desires. This section will prove enlightening to most, and the author hopes it will help those for whom business politics is a mystery. It really isn't very mysterious.

Section Four explains the concepts behind building a secure financial future for you and your family. Chapter 11 explains money and taxes. Know the definitions of terms. The charts illustrate the respective place in which one's accumulated stash of money and the corresponding privilege/burden of taxes are. Knowing how to grow money as well as spend money is more and more important as your life progresses to its end and your family needs develop into bigger and bigger monetary responsibilities. Know how to budget effectively the money you do have, reduce your debts no matter their origination, and develop insurance plans that are going to be helpful to you and your family. Each and all of these skill sets are hard-earned learning.

Chapter 12 will take some of the mystery out of 401(k), 403(b), and IRA investment strategies for your money. IRAs have myriad forms, pay out in differing ways, and you need to know the current possibilities while you watch what the Congress and in some cases state legislatures do to these benefits. None of the rules is carved in stone. These shelters are the most popular form of retirement option with most companies, so the more you understand them, the better position you are in to negotiate for yourself.

Chapter 13 is about your own or a family member's continuing education option as a good investment. The cost of going to school and the availability of loans and scholarships are charted. The availability of e-clinics and on-line education makes the process more comfortable; however, it does not reduce the cost of education that much, but it does add the convenience of going to school in your own home. In some cases it is more expensive than a traditional college education.

Chapter 14 explains retirement and what you need to have done before this time arrives in your life. What does retirement mean, how will you afford it, what responsibilities are likely to crop up in your advancing years that may cost more money than you have stored? Is traveling an option, continuing education, living on a fixed income, or beginning a charitable foundation if you have more money than you want or can spend? The real question is: are you prepared to retire to rather than from a previous life/career situation? Learn what the 47-48-49 life charts have to say about retirement by 2024.

Appendices

As in previous editions of *Career Development*, the appendices offer valuable additional information. They include:

A. Entrepreneur's Quiz
B. Personality Inventory
C. Letters
D. Market Value Determination Charts
E. Procrastination Defined
F. Glossary
G. Résumé Skill Words List, Sample Résumé
H. Budget
I. You and the Law

Acknowledgments

Because this is the fourth edition of CAREER DEVELOPMENT: *Strategies and Technologies for Career and Life Balance*, there are more and more people to acknowledge as sources of help, ideas, implementation of processes suggested, and learning. Uppermost in my list would be those students, graduates, and professional men and women that have been clients, friends, and family members and have taken my ideas and suggestions to heart and succeeded.

Students were the inspiration for the financial literacy section. The crazy mix of words they all thought they understood well until it came time to negotiate are all related to finance. Understanding how to negotiate well is a very important lifetime skill, and one gets better at it with practice.

A special debt of gratitude is due Professor Sally Baker of DeVRY Institute of Technology at Kansas City for her insight and suggestions about the tax section of Chapter 11. Professor Lynn Schuchman, also from DeVRY, KC, contributed to the ideas about retirement and what that would mean to graduates who are just beginning their life careers. Working with graduating students is especially rewarding because they more readily see with application how well these suggestions and ideas do work. Sean James, a former student/ graduate comes to mind as he continues to climb the corporate ladder and dream his dream of becoming a CEO. He is within two levels of that dream as I write this. Although he graduated February 2000, he continues to keep in touch and tell me about the successes that have come his way because "he got started on the right foot."

Most of all, my friends and associates who have understood on some level that I could not go to dinner, or to a movie, or off on a picnic junket, as I was working on my book, deserve a tremendous note of gratitude. It must be very frustrating to have someone become so unattainable and yet be so visibly present. Writing is not a group activity, and isolating oneself from others does not make and influence friends for the better, but it is a sacrifice I had to make and was willing to make to meet deadlines set by editors and others.

Although the mysteries of publication have eluded me these past 10 years of writing these texts, I would be sadly remiss if I did not thank Sande Johnson, the acquisitions editor, and assistant editor, Michelle Williams. They understand the labyrinthine ways of publishing. After this goes to copy, I am sure there will be others as there have been in the past; they just are not identified yet.

About the Author

Dr. Monica E. Breidenbach is the founder of Career Management Services in Prairie Village, Kansas, and currently a Senior Professor at DeVRY Institute of Technology in Kansas City, Missouri. Dr. Breidenbach has made her home in the Kansas City area since 1978 when she moved from Washington, D.C., where she was a senior counselor for a Washington, D.C.–based executive search firm, Pierson Associates. Upon arrival, she immediately began her counseling practice in the Kansas City area, which was extended at later dates to include an adjunct professorship at Ottawa University in Overland Park, Kansas, and subsequently a full professorship at DeVRY.

Dr. Breidenbach's current interests are developing materials for graduating college students to enable them to find the best possible job in the rich and developing markets for their talents and skills. In her private practice, she is redesigning her approach as "the coach in your corner" to extend to a variety of ways coaching may be needed by today's executives, professionals, and managers in their contemporary leadership roles.

Monica Breidenbach has authored, coauthored, and contributed to seven books and one K–12 series of texts with various publishers in the United States and England over the last 20 years. She continues to pen articles for magazines, newspapers, and the professional press in the field of career advancement and business management.

This newest book, CAREER DEVELOPMENT: *Strategies and Technologies for Career and Life Balance*, Fourth Edition, is her latest effort to provide college graduates with the best and most contemporary advice. This direction will create options to enable the graduates to find the choicest jobs available to them given their skills, talents, education, and experiences in life and work.

The text covers the search process from research to résumé writing, cyberspace résumé capabilities, CD-ROM business cards, interactive interviewing styles for all levels of interviewing, negotiations techniques that work, superior and focused marketing suggestions, advice about politics in the workplace, and a complete section on the financial literacy that will make terrific negotiators out of the graduates, who will then be ready to meet the future and continue on their roads to success and collect the appropriate rewards for their skills and talents.

Dr. Breidenbach has enabled thousands of students to achieve their dreams by encouraging them to follow the directives outlined in this new text. Her clients' success ratio in private practice is over 99 percent in the contemporary workplace of the last 5 years. She enables her clients to confront the problems and opportunities of today's workplace for the talented, educated, and gifted worker.

Reality— City on the Hill

F*ast Company*, with Roper Starch Worldwide, conducted an on-line survey in April 1999. It opened a window on the complex, convoluted, and sometimes even contradictory factors that people juggle while making choices that will affect their lives and careers.

In general, those surveyed felt they had a balance between their lives and careers (60% yes, 33% no, 7% not sure). In looking at whether or not they would want more balance between work life and personal life, the survey evaluated their willingness to accept some trade-offs, and the results were overwhelmingly in agreement (87% agree, 6% disagree, 6% not sure). Balance is a choice individuals make regarding life, career, and the harmony between the two. Often the world outside the home makes a balance hard to achieve.

Money is a big issue to all of us. Money is perceived as the most powerful factor in success on the job and in providing for homes and families. The next question would logically be, "How much money is enough?" Philosophers of antiquity, intellectuals of Renaissance eras in human development, and contemporary thinkers agree almost unilaterally that there is no such thing as "enough."

Everyone dreams, and those dreams fuel our desires to establish success in a field, create and maintain a family, have enough money to educate ourselves and our progeny, and reserve enough treasure for health and retirement developments. We Americans are a nation of strivers, entrepreneurs, developers, and pioneers. We have created a great nation, a rich nation, and in most local and foreign challenges, we act responsibly. Creating that dream revealed the struggle between the hope of fulfillment and the futility of not succeeding, which are continuing realities for a wide variety of ethnic, religious, and international immigrants.

Everyone dreams, and those dreams fuel our desires.

What we can learn from our national struggles to fulfill the American dream can be applied to each and every individual who is pursuing a personal dream of career success and intimate personal relationships. We first need or want and then we achieve *x*. When we get or spend what we have, we are balancing the life and career polar attractions that beckon us. No matter what it is that we have more of, when achieved that new possession or recognition will change the name of the game, and we will have new needs to balance and achieve a brand-new want.

This can result in a sense of personal freedom at some point for many. So the goal is to dream, work assiduously to achieve that dream, and contemplate the serendipitous aspirations that telescope beyond us on the road. We may end up on a different path in a much more fantastic place, but nothing will happen without the dream's initial pursuit.

The chart on the following page illustrates the polar opposites that we need to balance "for the good life."

Balance

World-class sages have all known and equated happiness and health with emotional stability and moderation in all things. The Greeks used *sôphrosunê* when they meant balance coupled with wisdom. The Romans used *temperantia* to mean the same kind of virtuous combination. Bart Simpson says, "Don't have a cow, man." Being surefooted and steady takes hard work, whether it be in personal relationships, career building, job searching, overcoming illness, and much more if we are trying to keep all of these in balance in our own lives.

Assertive individuals know how to express their feelings and desires, whereas aggressive individuals try to control other people's behaviors by using threats, implied or expressed. Neither is right or wrong, but the question is: which is more likely to be a workable strategy between two people or two groups?

We all need to pay attention to how we look to others. Do the colors you wear complement or distract? Is your style offensive or pleasing to others? Primping could lead to vanity if done to excess. If you suspect your attention to how you look is out of control, then set reasonable limits for your daily preparation and gradually reduce the time. If it takes you 2 hours to prepare to meet the public daily, try $1\frac{1}{2}$ hours and work your way down without injuring your reputation for good looks and a pleasing personality.

Workaholics do not work to achieve a goal. They work compulsively, often needlessly, believing that work of and by itself is virtuous. Concentration, on the other hand, draws us toward a common focus. "Self-worth is not measured in hours of overtime," according to Dr. Albert Ellis, New York psychologist.

Generosity is not a great virtue in present-day value systems. The fear of being generous is to be thought gullible, and no one wants to be considered exploitable. However, being generous means you know how and when to draw the line in a chance encounter and will go to help someone obviously in need of your assistance.

Avoid worrying that you might have the "disease of the week" as described on the news shows or on *ER* or *Chicago Hope* each week. While a temperature or bad cough may send a healthy person to the drugstore, hypochondriacs will be convinced that they are dying of some hidden malady related to a dreadful tuberculosis plague or possibly AIDS. If people who know you start to notify you that you are a bit over the edge about your health and projected illnesses, then take a good look at yourself. You may be on the edge.

UNDERSTANDING BALANCE	
In balance	**Out of balance**
Assertive	Aggressive
Beauty	Vanity
Concentration	Workaholic
Great-hearted	Gullible
Healthy	Hypochondriac
Optimist	Daydreamer
Polite	Discourteous
Risk taker	Foolhardy
Self-discipline	Rigid
Thrifty	Cheap

Optimists usually carry out and plan for the fulfillment of their dreams, whereas daydreamers just dream. Two people will look at a given job opportunity and each will think, "I can do that." Optimists will prepare for the interview by maybe taking a few extra classes to bone up on the topic or researching the company and its policies and enter the arena prepared for the interview. Daydreamers will just show up for the interview without any preparation or research and wonder why they are not chosen.

If there is one thing that separated John F. Kennedy, Jr., from all his contemporaries, it was his politeness. There is no group more nosy and in-your-face rude than the American press, and yet he treated each and every one of them politely. No matter how rude someone may be to you, you win if you maintain your composure and keep your cool. You don't have to answer anything you do not wish to discuss, but a short phrase to indicate that you are not going to go any further in the discussion complete with a smile is all that is needed.

Risks have their rewards, and successful gamblers measure the potential wins and losses before they take risks. Quitting your job with a rapier-sharp comment may satisfy your ego, but it is a reckless thing to do. You need references, and you never know when you may see these people again on your career path. You may be even more reckless if you have no job to go to, no money in the bank, and credit card debt or school loans bulging out of your portfolio. Think before you make any important move in your job or in life.

Optimists usually carry out and plan for the fulfillment of their dreams, whereas daydreamers just dream.

A frequent symbol used in Chinese cultural expressions is the bamboo plant, because it bends with the wind. The balanced person is able to do that also. The self-disciplined person knows how, when, and even how far to bend the rules to achieve a goal. The rigid personality is too tight and unforgiving even when personal life goals may be sacrificed.

Sensible people are thrifty individuals. They will use what resources they have to advantage and will not be afraid to spend their money, energy, or talent as needed. Some clues that you may be tight or considered so by others include the following: one, those close to you and frequently observant of your handling of money may resent your approach to not spending money. For example, you never pick up the check, and if possible, will always let someone else pay for your meal. Two, your contemporaries may not feel comfortable when you represent yourself as poorer than you are. There is no reason to be cheap.

Expectations

Collegians arrive at graduation with some false expectations about job searches, which need to be clarified at the outset.

EXPECTATION 1

Finding you a job upon graduation is someone else's responsibility, such as graduate placement offices, career centers, career counselors, generous professors, good friends, parents, and the like. Not so! What they can do is help.

Most schools provide a career center in which you can learn job searching skills, and you are encouraged to practice them while you are in your last term before graduation and with even more force upon graduation. There are many books on the market to help you. The Internet has a variety of sites where you can learn how to do self-assessment, design a résumé, develop a market plan, and search companies for potential job opportunities. Don't overlook the new and updated software programs that are also on the market for very reasonable prices.

Finding your first position after graduation is your job and no one else's, nor should you allow anyone to do it for you. Remember, you will be the one who has to go to work each day. Use all the advice and help you can find. Libraries in your school and in your neighborhood usually have career centers and equipment set up in a special place. You will find the librarians very helpful, if you know what you want to find. Most libraries are equipped with computers, which you can use to access research information and print the results. These computers are not interactive, but research and opportunities for printing the information acquired are available in abundance.

Many colleges provide a career-counseling center complete with identification boards for job listings that the school library may access for you. Often there are individuals called career counselors or career advisors. These men and women are very helpful if you ask for help. None of these people is responsible for finding you a job. That is your responsibility and yours alone.

Some schools organize job fairs. Take advantage of these opportunities to meet a variety of employers looking for recent graduates to hire. There will be many employers all located in one place, and their express purpose is to hire graduates. It is a great opportunity. Career fairs are conducted throughout the country in a variety of settings, so take advantage whenever you can. They usually are free for your participation, and they are an excellent place for you to find good connections to companies and jobs that interest you.

EXPECTATION 2

Your best option for jobs is your networking with the collegians graduating with you, or faculty members, or on-campus recruiters. Learning how to market yourself is a great set of skills that will provide you with job opportunities for the rest of your life. So learn how to do it well this first time. The opportunities are myriad: career fairs, networking with professional association members in the field you want to enter, checking out the people you work with in your job during school, mining the riches of the connections you have through your parents and family members, and last but not least, the alumni association—every school has one.

EXPECTATION 3

All graduates want to make a lot of money. Many graduates have a big loan or debt hanging over their heads. Thinking that this first job should be the best-paying option of your career is foolish. Yes, you have worked hard and it has cost a lot of money, time, sweat, and maybe tears to get this education. Set your priorities to build on your career skills and select the best opportunity that will expand your learning, strengthen your skills, and provide opportunities for you to learn even more. Graduation is not the end of the road but a beginning, so select carefully in order to be able to grow to your full potential.

When your dream to achieve a degree is fulfilled, you will want to find work that pays you well, respects your skill and experience, uses your education, and demands you seek more certification. But the real key here will be that you are doing something you like and have been doing something that engages you intellectually since the day you graduated. No career builds better than that kind. In most surveys that ask people what means the most to them in their work, the top responses almost always include job satisfaction. There is nothing more gratifying, even money.

Success

Human history is replete with examples of individuals who have "made it" and then they crash. Why is this? I believe it is because we have the wrong definition of success or a limited vision of our potential. We all know people who are excellent at everything they do, but probably are not monomaniacally devoted to one career path or one obsessive idea.

His contemporaries called the Greek thinker Diogenes "the Cynic." One day Alexander the Great visited him. Alexander listed all his achievements to date and the pursuits of additional conquests he planned for the future. When he finished, Diogenes asked him, "And then what?" To which Alexander replied, "Then I will be able to relax and enjoy this life." Diogenes responded, "Why not save yourself a lot of trouble by relaxing and enjoying yourself now?"

Success is about who you are, not what you possess.

Alexander never did get the point. Many college graduates and other job seekers are a lot like Alexander in pursuit of their lofty goals. Those who enjoy the most success in life are able to find satisfaction in the journey, not just upon arrival at the end of the road. Do you work to satisfy your weekend needs, or can you enjoy your work and your weekend pleasures with balance and excellence? Pursuing excellence is difficult but not totally elusive if you plan carefully and do not have unrealistic expectations.

Success is not wealth or power. Success is excellence and fulfillment. Success is about who you are, not what you possess. Discover your talents; they are many. Develop your talents and skills because they can only continue to become better within you. Then serve as many other occupants of the planet as you can while you exercise your accumulated skills and talents.

Spirituality

You read it correctly, spirituality. Spirituality in the workplace? Yes. Today we know that people and companies do well, even fantastically well, when their values match. I urge you to go beyond the bottom line, the quarterly reports, and seek answers to long-term questions about the company's behavior in the marketplace.

Individuals also need to measure whether their efforts for the business they serve are doing something to change the world. Is there a near possibility, if you cooperate with the corporate goals of the organization, that together you may change the world? If not, your spirituality may be in jeopardy while toiling for a company whose values you do not hold. To find a company with parallel values to your own requires effort, research, and a clear understanding of your own values. If an organization claims it focuses on integrity, responsibility, and transparent ethical criteria, where is the proof? These certainly are spiritual dimensions, and if they can be substantiated by the research available about the company's activities in the marketplace, this may be the place for you.

To be prepared to search in this manner may require you to simplify your life a bit. We all live in a fast-paced, ear to the cell phone, consumer-driven, modern-day environment. Knowing what is most important to you is the key to simplifying your life. No one else can do this for you.

Step one: Know what is right for you. Pay no attention to people who want you to veer off in their direction and where they think you should be headed.

Know your core values and apply them in your lifestyle .

Step two: Know your core values and apply them in your lifestyle no matter what fashion says is the leading edge of life in the fast lane. Step three: If you are investing your time and hard-earned money, be sure you understand what it is you are gaining. Once these three steps are uppermost in your mind, simplifying your life will be a breeze. The accent is on you, not on what others think about you or want for you.

In today's literature there are a lot of commentators who are urging people to slow down, think things through, develop communities for support at the workplace and at home. If you panic when you wake up each day, how can you look forward to what the day may offer? If you have been there, done that, and don't want to stay there, then you will have to assess where you want to be. The past is not always a predictor of the future, but it usually is a good touchstone. Monetary and spiritual rewards can be available every day. We need to look, be sensitive to our own needs, be willing to explore new options, and probe new ways of thinking out of the box.

- First, remember that time, energy, even fantasies, as well as money, are assets to be used to attain identified goals.

- Second, put family and friends first. So far no one on his or her deathbed has been heard to say, "I should have spent more time at my office desk." Even Scrooge finally got the message.

- Third, freelance a bit to test the waters, and if it works for you, do it. You will be in charge of your day, your clients, your business activity, and your coming and going. You will work hard, but you will be doing what you want to do.

- Fourth, consider that a dollar saved is worth $1.40 you won't have to earn in the future, assuming a 28% tax bracket. Wealth is having more than you need; poverty is not having enough. Before you purchase something, ask yourself, "If I didn't need this yesterday, why do I need it today?"

- Fifth, turn debts into investments (see Chapter 11). Prepay an additional mortgage payment per year, and you'll save $20,000 interest over the life of your mortgage. Pay credit card debt as quickly as you can; it is imperative.

- Sixth, consult with someone who is knowledgeable about how to plan for a financial future. College is not a parental responsibility but an investment in your future. You are in charge, so what matters is how much you think you will need to retire, not what the financial planners want you to invest. How about considering a working retirement? When you need to draw down from your nest egg, go ahead. You do not need to leave a big estate. Your children can manage for themselves, and should.

Why am I encouraging you to slow down, smell the roses, love your family and friends, and be an excellent worker, but not necessarily an obsessed worker? It is important because depression is a critical workplace problem today. More managers report having to deal with mental health issues among their charges. A two-to-one differential exists between small organizations reporting depression and larger organizations (17% little or no problems to 8% in larger organizations). See for yourself: **www.treatdepression.com/workplace/home.htm.**

Provide time, space, and opportunity for yourself and your loved ones to succeed where it really counts, in relationships and in accomplishments. You can balance home and work, but it will take consciousness, awareness, sensitivity, and communication with and among all involved.

Take the leap and try from this new beginning with your degree and your new professional job, and make it work for all who know and love you as well as satisfying the work demands that you are willing to take on your shoulders. Even though the bulk of this book is about how to locate the best possible position for yourself after graduation, I continue to caution you about keeping on track managing the things that really matter in your life.

Résumés

These are the basic tools needed to prepare for a quality career search: first, gather your professional background information and assemble the data in one place. Second, select a single résumé format for your professional version—black print on a white $8^1/_2$" by 11" sheet. Third, develop a variety of formats to enter the complete marketplace with cyberspace options.

Résumé background information is vital to get a correct focus on where you have been and where you wish to go in your professional career. This information will help flesh out your résumé information so that the reader can get a reasonable verbal picture of your readiness for the business job market of choice.

Résumé formats are built to meet the variety of needs in the market today. A professional-looking, $8^1/_2$" by 11" page for the traditional reader is the mark of a sensitive job searcher. An ASCII text version of this same résumé text for international distribution on the Internet gives global access to your presentation of credentials and skills. Sending a résumé over the Internet communicates that the sender is Net savvy, which may be a desire of the potential employer when hiring new colleagues.

Cyberspace formats are limited only to the imagination and programming abilities of the author. Depending on your accumulated skills in formatting, use of programming techniques, and the availability of commercial programs that may be within your reach, the variety, length, and breadth of these formats clearly demonstrate to the recipient your technical skills along with whatever you have listed on your résumé. The image agrees with the word. Claiming technical literacy and demonstrating it on your résumé are two different things. Employers notice when both are present.

CHAPTER 1

Résumé Information Research

This chapter is very important because employers have noted that when they ask employees why they are leaving in an exit interview, 40 percent of those employees say things like, ". . . the job didn't fit," 26 percent indicate that they found more money, 18 percent leave for personal or family reasons—usually without enumerating what those reasons might entail—and 11 percent quit because they could not get along with the manager or a coworker. This survey was conducted by Caliper, headquartered in Princeton, New Jersey. The participants were a cross section of people in management, sales, customer service, technical, and administrative positions.

The job fit is parallel to your education, credentials, skill bases, and past work experience. If you have this data gathered somewhere, now is the time to locate it and review its relevance to the development of your new résumé. A good résumé is not a rewrite of a previous résumé but a completely new look at your readiness for the market of your choice.

Résumés

Résumés and letters are important to have already available for your use. Save them to a disk, and they will be ready when you need them. You will need a group of cover letters for the following purposes: ad answering letter, inquiry letters to peers and decision makers, broadcast letters, and a model marketing letter or minirésumé. A description of the content of each of these letters is in Appendix C. Most exchange is over the Internet these days, so sharpen your Internet skills and look around before you take the leap into a company.

Several Internet sites are listed at the end of this chapter, and others will become available to you as you go to these various sites. Don't overlook the company's own Web site; just remember that the site is used for their marketing purposes when you are looking at the information. You are looking for contacts and job availability when you read their information.

Now that you will earn or have earned a degree or ongoing certification in your field, your résumé should look remarkably different.

Information credentials you need to gather are

- complete degree history with transcripts of education credits and grades and list of honors
- most recent certification
- educational seminars and workshops that you attended
- at least two prior work experiences whereby your skills were developed and enhanced
- a skills list that is current, not a wish list of who you hope to become, but who you are
- reviews of former managers, promotions, and special citations you may have earned

Go to any one of the sites located at the end of this chapter for assistance in self-assessment techniques. A number of software programs are also available. In Appendix B of this text is a short personality profile inventory you might find helpful in pulling together who you are and describing that on a one-page résumé for a total stranger.

In addition to the hard data that will be available from all the credentials you can pull together, there are your soft skills. These may be harder to define, but will be the main reason you are fired if you don't have them. People are hired for the skills, education, and certifications they have earned, but they are usually fired because of some personality dissatisfaction that employers no longer think is worth their skills, education, and talent. This is sometimes referred to as *emotional intelligence.*

Soft Skills

Emotional intelligence includes self-awareness, self-regulation, motivation, empathy, and a host of social skills. We all think we know what these skills are, but let's take a look at them on a deeper level than their dictionary definitions.

SELF-ASSESSMENT

Do you know yourself well enough to trust your evaluation of your abilities, or do you go looking for a gimmick quiz or fill-in-the-blanks outline of employee soft skills? Do you have a good image of yourself and a clear sense of self-confidence based on self-knowledge? This soft skill will make you a good decision maker. Have you learned from your experience that you can trust your gut feelings and intuition about what is going on in a situation? This requires some collective wisdom and true self-evaluation. Check out your assumptions with someone who knows you well, and see if the person agrees with what you think is a good and accurate self-awareness.

Do you have a good image of yourself and a clear sense of self-confidence based on self-knowledge?

SELF-CONTROL

Handling and managing one's emotional reactions to events is a learned process, and some have learned more than others have. This is so important today because a group of the working population, at least in the United States, is often close to despair and depression, to say nothing of the stress overload you and your coworkers bring to the job daily. Add to this group your customers and your suppliers, and you have your hands full, even if you are not the manager.

If you practice self-control, it makes you more responsible and timely in your reactions to others. You don't need to gratify every feeling you have on the spot. You can control your behavior, but remember that you surely cannot control anyone else's. If you show self-control, people will trust you to do what is right, believe that you will act in everyone's best interest, trust your judgment, and have confidence that you will not be overwhelmed by the moment or the situation. You can handle things well.

MOTIVATION

Motivation is a personal skill. Those who feel they can motivate others by punishment or reward have missed the boat over the past 50 years. What psychology has taught us is that we are each our own best motivators. Those who are self-motivated make good employees, great team players, and often outstanding supervisors.

This soft skill powers the drive toward excellence because it is self-driven. We are willing to set challenging goals and will take intelligent risks that are in our own best interest. Others observe our behavior and our optimism and are often encouraged to go and do likewise, although this is no guarantee because the self is the mover here.

EMPATHY

Empathy is something we all appreciate in others. It is a concern for others' feelings. "I may be wrong, but let me down easy and I'll be more encouraged to change." The possessor of empathy, when confronted with someone who is stressed to the limits, will often say, "How can I help?" Just the fact that someone is willing to help is often enough to snap someone out of their doldrums.

If you have this skill and continue to develop it, you will find you are wanted on all teams. People like you because they feel empowered by your empathy regarding them and their dilemmas. Reading the emotional currents in a work setting is very valuable whether you are the manager or a team member. Lives may be saved!

SOCIAL SKILLS

This group of skills is vital, and yet we leave most schoolhouses without ever being introduced to them. Formerly these skills came from the home and parental guidance, but today's families are so disparate, and socialization with each other is often neither a goal nor a desire. No wonder our total society is so coarse.

Social skills reveal the ability to handle relationships adeptly. People with social skills usually are persuasive and influential. Brilliant ideas go nowhere when the idea hatcher has the social skills of a snail. Leadership is the usual result of possessing social skills. People can be inspired by and will take guidance from someone who knows how to talk with them and clearly delineate what is expected or even willing to accept a challenge because of the way in which it is presented.

CAN YOU IMPROVE?

Of course you can as long as you are not pushing up daisies yet. Know what your strengths and weaknesses are. What are you good at and what needs work? Is the skill set important enough to you to merit the work it takes to improve? You may like to hear piano music, but you do not want to go to the work of learning to play the piano. When you decide to improve your social skills or any emotional skills, go easy and take your time. Those individuals who are good at a certain task have been at it for a long time, and you may be just beginning.

Treat all your mistakes as a pool of opportunities to learn something about yourself.

There are good role models. Public figures, teachers, counselors, some coaches, parents, neighbors, TV talking heads, and movies about relationships, among others, are all sources to learn about how to improve one's emotional skills strengths. Ask trusted friends or family members to help you by telling you when you are missing the mark and when you have successfully moved into a new level of achievement.

Signs of improvement are usually endorsed by a manager's reviews of your work. Look for the emotional ways your manager is suggesting you might improve your relationships with coworkers, other department heads, people you don't like, and customers. Treat all your mistakes as a pool of opportunities to learn something about yourself and as an additional rung on your ladder to better relationships. Don't give up when you think you have failed; just ask yourself, "What can I learn from this?" There is an answer. Practice makes perfect, and you have a lifetime to improve. See the Rutgers University Consortium on Emotional Intelligence at their Web site (**www.linkageinc.com/ei99/keynotes.htm**).

Career Fairs

Career fairs are a modern-day phenomena, which are very helpful to searchers. Companies gather in groups of 30–150 to investigate what is available in a community that will enable them to do their work better. They are ready to hire new people, so go to the fairs with 50 copies of your résumé. Have the group assembled scouted before you enter the arena. The company sponsoring the fair will give you a list of the participants, and you should settle on where you can best spend your time at the fair. Call ahead of the day of the fair.

First, select those companies you know you want to work for and would be thrilled to get a job interview with someone in the organization. Second, go to those companies whose names and logos are mysteries to you. Find out what they do and decide later what to do with the information. Leave a copy of your résumé if you are impressed with who they are and what they do. Third, if you have time, go to the remaining companies that are there. You may be surprised at the new things you can find out about companies you thought you knew well, including your own current company.

Career fairs are not for hiring as much as they are for informational interviews for you to make contacts, share résumés and business cards, and then call within 24 hours to make an appointment if what you learned is related to what you are looking for in your new career. Often sales recruiters, which is usually who covers a company's booth at these fairs, can tell you a lot about their company's future, because sales is about the future. These people usually know more than most of the regular employees in the firm about the company's future.

Doing on-line research is the most helpful tool available to the job searcher today.

Doing on-line research is the most helpful tool available to the job searcher today. Knowing who you are and what your skills are will go a long way to finding a job that fits you. Formulating a well-presented professional résumé makes it easier to translate it into ASCII text and whatever cyberspace formats you wish to use. Taking your résumés to a career fair is to your advantage. Go often, but know what group of companies are attending the fair so as not to waste precious time.

Continuing Research

The following resources are made available to the reader rather than the traditional end-of-chapter questions to be answered in groups or individually. These are resources that the author used as research materials and are made available to the reader. The Web references were available at the time of printing, but as Web sites go may have been replaced by better resources by the time the reader gets this text. Go with the flow of data and sources. When prices are quoted, they are from **www.amazon.com**.

Light reading, anyone?

Books

Cooper, Robert K., Ph.D., and Ayman Sawaf. *Executive IQ: Emotional Intelligence in Leadership Organizations*. New York: Grosset-Putman. 1998.

Goleman, Daniel. *Working with Emotional Intelligence*. New York: Bantam Books. 1998.

Weisenger, Hendrie, Ph.D. *Emotional Intelligence at Work*. San Francisco: Jossey-Bass. 1998.

Journals

Waldrop, James, and Timothy Butler. "Eight Failings that Bedevil the Best." *Fortune*. November 23, 1998. Pages 293–294.

___. "Finding the Job You Should Want." *Fortune*. March 2, 1998. Pages 211+.

www.workforceonline.com

Try these sites

General Web Site Search

www.askjeeves.com

(Ask a question and you will get many options to consider)

www.altavista.com

(Topic search with the fewest words possible)

www.dogpile.com

(Search engine of search engines)

www.google.com

(Search engine by keywords)

Résumé Research Web Sites

www.about.com

Professional Résumé Writing

Four Résumé Tools for Job Search

Résumé Bank

Career Mosaic Writing Center

Lifestyle Quiz

Interest Finder Quiz

Mock Interview

Stress-o-Meter

Team Player Quiz

Work Style Quiz

www.acareer.com

www.compuware.com/careers/resbuild

(Compuware's Online Résumé Builders)

www.law.univ.edu/Student_Services

(The Success Checklist. FIRST YEAR. Clarify who you are and what you want. SIGI Computerized Guidance System.)

www.lycos.com/careers/careerguide/resume.html

(Lycos Career Guide for Winners: helpful feedback, searches, mail)

www.kappabetasigma.org/pbs_resumetip.html

(PBS Résumé Builders)

Got a few extra bucks?

Software Programs

ResumeMaker Deluxe CD-ROM. Pleasanton, CA: Individual Software, Inc. 1999. **www.mgendron@individualsoftware.com** ($25.00)

Create Résumés Quick and Easy. Pleasanton, CA: Individual Software, Inc. 1995. This is the same company, but the software only writes résumés. ($20.00)

CHAPTER 2

Résumé Formulae

How a résumé looks is a reflection of your professionalism and at the same time gives clues about your technical excellence in its preparation. There are hardware tools and software programs that are a big help in producing a professional-looking résumé. Another tool that is most helpful is the Internet and its access to universities and college sites where you can get help and see examples of résumés and letters that are appropriate to a job search.

However, I want to caution you to avoid those box-type services that make your résumé and everyone else's look the same. Customize your résumé, and if that is not possible with the software or Internet site you are using, then move to another one. (Several are suggested at the end of this chapter.)

Résumé Content

What belongs on the résumé and what is superfluous need addressing at this juncture. You have all your data. Now, how and where does it go to get the best benefit for you? Résumés are to be read, and unless they get before the decision maker and are read by that individual, you have wasted your time. Make the résumé read like a marketing piece. That is what it is. If you have created a sharp and focused résumé, it will impress the recipient.

A résumé has two purposes for existence. One is to get the attention of a decision maker so that you can set an appointment to discuss the options available.

Make the résumé read like a marketing piece .

Two, the résumé is a tool for two strangers to begin conversation about what both parties are interested in discussing. Usually after you have set the appointment and have been ushered into the decision maker's office, conversation begins. Remember your social skills as well as trying to keep your nervousness under control. In about 5–6 minutes, you will notice the interviewer puts your résumé aside. The opportunity for your résumé to impress has passed at that point. Positive or negative impressions remain.

If the person is positively impressed, you will be given an extended interview (over 20 minutes), introduced to other staff and business associates, invited to come back for another interview, scheduled to take some technical test, invited to lunch, or extended an opportunity to sit in on a staff meeting. The decision maker has been impressed. If you are ushered out the door quickly, the decision maker is not impressed. However, you should remain courteous and move your social skills into high gear so that you leave a good impression. You could be called back for a different open position simply because you were so impressive. Don't lose your cool!

Résumé Information

What should your résumé say about you? First, it should list your identification so that you can be reached if the interviewer needs to call you or arrange for another meeting with you. Second, the most important section of your résumé is your statement of a career objective. This enables the interviewer to see if you are headed in the same direction as the company considering hiring you. A complete career objective has three parts: (1) three industries that interest you, (2) three skills sets you possess at the time, and (3) demonstration of how these skills will be of benefit to the company.

Third, provide a skills profile in which you arrange your three skill sets into columns as they were identified in your career objective. These three columns contain a breakdown of each skill set, for example, management is the skill set. Your expertise within that set may include scheduling, training, supervision, and Microsoft Office. This columnar arrangement enables the reader to see at a glance what predominant skills you bring to the table.

Fourth, identify your educational support for these skills and fifth, identify your work experiences for these skills. Remember: a résumé is not your life history. It is a one-page assessment of your readiness for the market of your choice.

The content should be listed in the following order:

Identification. Information (right, left, or centered at the top of the page).

Career Objective. See explanation under the Résumé Information section above.

Skills Profile. Three columns for clarity and ease of sight.

Education. Current degree and go backward from there. Delineate how the chosen courses were helpful in supporting your skills set. For example, identifying Principles of Management or Project Management would be in line with the previously stated Skills Profile set, Management.

Experience. Last two jobs, current and backward from there. Identify years only, not months. Select those responsibilities held that support the skill sets (new employee training, night supervision).

Material to Use

Use only 20 lb. paper, the blackest ink on the whitest paper, 8½″ x 11″ sheets. Select your paper and envelopes at the same time. One ream of paper and 250 number 10 envelopes will serve you nicely. If using color, restrict yourself to ivory, pewter, or beige. Never use pastel colors.

Curriculum Vitae

European nations and Japan use the *curriculum vitae* (Latin, the course of [one's] life) as the résumé for many positions. This Latin title refers to medieval times when professors needed to support their request for a teaching position by printing the total summary of their academic achievements for the chancellor of the college to evaluate. This summary would be pages long and considered better the more pages it had. Academe, government jobs, and some diplomatic core positions still require the *curriculum vitae*.

In American business, a one-page résumé is all that the modern business leader wants to read when considering whether to meet with a prospective candidate for a position or not. Some European nations are also moving to this one-page concept for a résumé. When Japanese companies want a *curriculum vitae*, they have a format they want you to follow. Do so. When presenting your credentials to another country where the native tongue is not English, have your résumé printed in that country's language on one side and in English on the other.

In American business, a one-page résumé is all that the modern business leader wants to read.

The same is true for business cards you want to present in your search proceedings. Business cards should not be cluttered with more information than is necessary. Your name, day or evening phone, fax numbers, e-mail addresses, and company name should be sufficient. Only give out your business card when professionals ask you for it or offer you their business card. Do not shuffle and pass cards out at a meeting or a luncheon you are attending. Just be prepared to distribute cards to those who are interested enough to ask for one. When you receive a business card, soon thereafter jot a note on the back so you will remember why you have this individual's card.

Business Profiles

Business profiles are available for companies on their own Web sites. They can also be accessed from other Web sites such as **www.hoovers.com.** A list of sites is included at the end of this chapter. Know the company where you are interviewing. A 1999 commercial reveals a very telling picture of a candidate at a dinner who is not prepared and answers more and more foolishly as the dinner progresses. It is an ad for hoovers.com, and it really tells the tale straight. If you are not prepared to know the information that is readily available, you will be considered unprepared for the interview and negatively evaluated by the decision maker. In addition you will have embarrassed yourself unbelievably. Today there is no excuse for not knowing a lot about the company you are interviewing.

There is no excuse for not knowing a lot about the company you are interviewing.

YOUR PREPARATION

Take advantage of the experts on the Web telling you all you really need to know. Use a good software program to put your résumé together. Most good software packages provide a way for you to keep track of your search. You need to keep track of your contact sources, a calendar of events, and copies of frequently written letters and thank-you notes. These notes are sent within 24 hours after each interview to all who were at the interview. How you organize them is up to you, but if you do not have some order, you will forget whom you saw, what company, what follow-up is expected, and for what purpose. Your letters will sound bland and out-of-the-book rather than fresh and sincere.

Résumé Formats

Résumés are also built to emphasize different approaches to the job market. The common distinctions are described here.

CHRONOLOGICAL RÉSUMÉ

The oldest and most traditional of résumé formats. Someone who wants to stay in the same field uses it. The accent is on career focus or career objective. The skills, education, and experience support the career focus. Experience precedes education when experience is the more recent of the two. Stress accomplishments and professional affiliations.

FUNCTIONAL RÉSUMÉ

The functional resume is used when entering a new field or moving to a different geographical area. This résumé highlights functional skills in lieu of a goal statement. Accent is on a career objective or career goal, which identifies three industries of interest and draws focus to three specific skills sets. The skills profile, education, and experience support the three skill sets. This résumé format would suit a person with a strong managerial background, a developer or designer of software, a recent graduate, or a newcomer to a city.

LINEAR RÉSUMÉ

This résumé is an updated version of the chronological résumé, which includes paragraphs rather than marketing-type statements for career objective or focus statement. Skills profile columns may be bulleted for emphasis and visual impact. Employment accents position titles, responsibilities, achievements, and promotions. Educational credentials usually close this résumé.

ACHIEVEMENT RÉSUMÉ

This résumé is targeted with a sharp and clearly focused objective. Rather than a skills summary, more definition is given to the job target pursued. Supportive data includes capabilities, skills, and achievements that highlight preparedness for the job target. This resume usually closes with a short employment history and educational credentials.

PERFORMANCE RÉSUMÉ

Highlights the candidate's performance levels so far in a career track. Accent is on concisely stated accomplishments. Description of skill levels is necessary. Published authors, individuals with concentrated career data in midlevel management, inventors, or hardware developers will most likely use a performance résumé.

The most helpful thing to remember about each résumé is to customize it every time to the specific job market. The reader wants to be intrigued and impressed. Copying a format from a book or redoing an old résumé never works well for a candidate with a newly minted degree. After you have spent all that money, time, and energy on a degree, why shortchange yourself with an impoverished résumé? You are the only one who will lose if you do.

How the résumé looks is the most important thing when creating a marketing piece. Remember: This résumé is not your life history.

- Stay focused on the career objective. Everything must support the career objective.

- Avoid information glut. No one will read a multipage résumé in today's U.S. job market.

- Don't be afraid of white space. Leave room for people to make notes. Fill about three-quarters of the page with words and leave the rest open. Also, the résumé will be easier to read.

- Make sure it looks good. Test it with other people. What do they think of your résumé? (This is a measure of your ability to communicate your professionalism to a complete stranger.)

Continuing Research

Continue as you did for Chapter 1. There are repeat sources here because the two chapters are much alike for resource materials.

Light reading, anyone?

Journals

Waldrop, James, and Timothy Butler. "Finding the Job You Should Want." *Fortune.* March 2, 1998. Pages 211–214.

www.workforceonline.com

www.fastcompany.com

Try these sites

General Web Site Search

www.askjeeves.com

www.altavista.com

www.dogpile.com

www.google.com

Résumé Research Web Sites

www.about.com

　　Career Mosaic Writing Center

　　College Connections Résumé Writing Center

　　Résumé Bank (Global University Web)

　　Sample Résumé

　　Stress-o-Meter

www.acareer.com

www.compuware.com/careers/resbuild

　　(Compuware's Online Résumé Builders)

www.lycos.com/careers/careerguide/resume.html

www.kappabetasigma.org/pbs_resumetip.html

　　(PBS Résumé Builders)

Got a few extra bucks?

Software Programs

ResumeMaker Deluxe CD-ROM. Pleasanton, CA: Individual Software, Inc. 1999. **www.mgendron@individualsoftware.com** ($25.00)

Create Resumes Quick and Easy. Pleasanton, CA: Individual Software, Inc. 1995. This is the same company, but the software only writes résumés. ($20.00)

CHAPTER 3

Cyberspace Résumés

Cyberspace résumés are those résumés that depend on technology to be sent to potential employers when a graduate is in an active career search. These résumés reveal the technical knowledge and skills potential employees may have, not because they say so on their résumé, but because they have demonstrated technical skill in the formulation and communication of their résumé. Demonstrating technical skills while writing one's résumé cuts down on the exaggeration and lying that seem endemic in the searching world today; up to 40 percent of résumés contain lies, according to some estimates.

When a Cyberspace Résumé Is Needed

The place where cyberspace résumés are effective is on the Web. One needs to write the best possible résumé, post it with the most effective posting companies, and then choose among the options that are brought to your own computer. You need a smart résumé. What follows are some tips for reformatting your résumé to go online.

For résumés that go on the Web, convert verbs to nouns because digital eyeballs scan Web résumés. A human resources professional's eyeballs scanned the traditional résumé. Today's digital scanners are looking for job titles, technical and soft skills, educational levels, degrees, certification, and experience with software programs and product development; all are usually stated as nouns.

For résumés that go on the Web, convert verbs to nouns because digital eyeballs scan Web résumés.

Buzzwords are important. Those companies that use applicant tracking systems rank résumés by the number of keywords in them. If the company is looking for an accountant, they will take the one who uses Lotus 1-2-3, Microsoft Excel, and Peachtree First Accounting. The ranking system will tell them which individuals have all three or only one of these software programs in their experience. Know the keywords in your industry, education, and certification in order to maximize their use on the résumé.

Tracking systems can select personality traits, your soft skills, and your attitude. Identify your behavioral characteristics so that your passion will show and can be counted. Examples include enthusiasm, dependability, responsibility, and high energy level. Avoid tired language at all costs.

If you link your résumé to your personal Web page, then more detailed information can be made available to any decision maker who wants to find it. Make sure your home page is not mucked up with pictures of you, your favorite dog, or seasonal pictures of your family. The decision maker is not looking for pretty faces but for great skills.

Think of formatting your résumé as though you were creating a movie trailer about your readiness for the industries of your choice. Within 20 lines you must grab the attention of the reader or they will click away to a more interesting site. Lead with the assurance that you have the solutions to someone's problem. Assure them they can no longer work successfully without you on their team.

The one-page rule does not apply to the on-line world. As long as you have their interest, they will continue to scroll and read your information. At some point they do print your résumé, so make sure it will not exceed three printed pages.

One size or format does not fit all. Everyone needs at least four formats to actively make use of on-line capabilities and be ready for anyone who wants your résumé. This means that at all times you must have copies of or access to (1) one $8\frac{1}{2}'' \times 11''$ professional one-page résumé ready for distribution; (2) a word processing document of that professional résumé available for fax or e-mail clip-ons; (3) ASCII text or text-only file of the original résumé for ready distribution on the Net; and (4) an HTML-coded file copy with links, if you have a home page that is acceptable for professional viewing. No mechanic carries just one screwdriver. You have one résumé for content and the same information in a variety of formats for presentation.

Remember that scanners are reading your résumé. They are more sensitive to certain fonts or typefaces such as Helvetica, Courier, Futura, Optima, Palatino, New Century Schoolbook, and Times. The best typing size is between 10–14 points. Look at the font size after you type it. Try printing it in various type sizes, and see which one looks the best to you. If you use a fax to send your résumé, be sure to set the machine to fine mode. This way you will get a higher-quality printout on the receiving end.

Because e-mail attachments are considered an annoyance to many decision makers, they don't go to the trouble to read them. If you are sending your résumé by e-mail, paste the résumé version into the e-mail message rather than clip it on as an attachment. Companies worry about viruses, and they don't want to waste time with files their computers cannot translate.

If you are sending your résumé by e-mail, paste the résumé version into the e-mail message rather than clip it on as an attachment.

When a company or posting firm asks you for a subject line, respond with a theatre marquee thumbnail version of your readiness for the market. Sell yourself! Don't ignore your software's wizard. Most software programs have good résumé format options. The one caution I would suggest is that you avoid those that look like your résumé is a canned version rather than a custom-built résumé.

When using the Internet, target your résumé as precisely as possible. All these wizard assistants, font availability, and "Mercury-like" transmissions cannot make up for a misspelled word or an incorrect grammatical phrase. Use the spell checker and the grammar checker, but then recheck the résumé yourself. Have someone else read it who has never seen it, and see if they can find any problems. Then read it out loud. Often this will help with ungrammatical phrases. If you read the information from the end to the beginning, it will help you identify some of your spelling errors, because you are not trying to understand the content in any logical order.

Preparation of electronic documents is best spaced by staying in between the document's margin set at 65 characters per line. For example, 12.5-point Courier corresponds to 6.5-inch line length. This will enable your text to be protected from improper forced line inserts when the receiving program inserts them in their version. Mail the ASCII text to yourself to see how it looks on your monitor. Be sure that anything you mail—snail mail, fax, or e-mail—you have sent to yourself so you can see what happens to it and if it is being transmitted the way you want it to be received.

LIST OF GUIDELINES AND SUGGESTIONS FOR AN ELECTRONIC (OR ANY) RÉSUMÉ

- Be flawless.
- Be specific.
- Identify what you can do for the decision maker.
- An employer takes 30 seconds to scan a résumé. Make them count.
- Emphasize your skills.
- Use keywords and buzzwords.
- Use action words effectively.
- Highlight key points—capital letters, quotation marks, asterisks for emphasis.
- Formulate accurate information summaries.
- List only recent information.

- Quantify experience.
- Be organized, logical, and concise.
- Communicate enthusiastically.
- No salary information or queries about salary should appear with your résumé.
- Describe yourself personally yet professionally.
- Communicate honestly.
- Sell yourself.
- Personality should match position.
- Be consistent.
- Everything should look balanced and neat.

Business Cards

Almost all business cards have a blank back. When you have cards printed, list your skills, your previous job titles, your educational credentials, and certification or licenses you have earned on the back. Don't list all of these, but one or two give the reader a better idea of who you are and what you can do.

There is a new phenomenon in today's market. It is the CD-ROM business card. These cards come in different sizes and shapes; can be printed in the spectrum of colors; hold up to 40 MB of interactive multimedia, sound, and video; and they play in a standard CD-ROM drive. It is claimed that these cards are 10 times more effective than a conventional business card and will be noticed 10 times more. Once these are distributed, there will be no trouble attracting these readers to your business Web site. See end-of-chapter listing for access to some companies that are producing these CD-ROM business cards.

Web Site Designs

The principles of design do not change just because you are using the Web. The main principle of design is simplicity. This implies you have thought out your agenda carefully and have sketched, preferably on paper, your ideas about who you are, what your purpose is in going on the Web, and where the reader can find information and gain access to your information. Have the content arranged logically. If you need help, purchase a book, take a seminar, or follow the rules of your software as in Netscape Navigator Communicator.

On-Line Job Hunting

Does it work? *Fortune* magazine did a survey in July 1999. The results are rather supportive of the idea that this kind of approach to the market works.

2.5 million	Estimated number of résumés posted on the Internet
28,500	Estimated number of Web sites that offer job posting services
56%	Percentage of on-line job seekers who are not engineers or computer professionals
$105 million	Amount employers spent on on-line recruiting, 1998
$1.7 billion	Amount employers will spend on on-line recruiting, 2003 (projected)
17%	Percentage of *Fortune* Global 500 companies actively recruiting on the Internet, January 1, 1998
45%	Percentage of *Fortune* Global 500 companies actively recruiting on the Internet, January 1, 1999
81%	Percentage of résumés Cisco Systems receives via the Web
66%	Percentage of new hires at Cisco who come from the Web
68	Days shaved off Cisco's hiring cycle by using the Internet

(Source: Useem, Jerry. "For Sale Online: You." *Fortune*, July 5, 1999. pp. 67–78.)

Networking on the World Wide Web (WWW) is the newest, fastest, most responsive way of locating a great position available to today's graduates. Electronic advertising costs companies a lot less money to locate recruits for their open positions than the more traditional media does. The network is making it cost-efficient. This kind of ad attracts more qualified and technical professionals. Recruits are identified with lightning speed. The competition intensifies among companies to locate the best and the brightest.

Candidates need to match that capability by making their technical and qualified skills known to potential companies. In order to gain a competitive edge, graduates must be able to use a diversified approach to their job searching. Use both the larger and smaller electronic bulletin boards, especially those highlighting industries of interest. Posting your résumé with several posting companies is imperative.

You may have trained yourself to ignore banner ads, but look carefully because some companies are using banner ads to announce their job openings. Go to company Web sites. Probe deeply enough, and you will come to their job listings. In addition, many search engines provide a wide variety of services that list jobs from many companies, which you can compare in one site. The best among these are the oldest: Career Mosaic, The Monster Board, Online Career Center, Yahoo, and AltaVista. If you want to be surprised, select **www.dogpile.com,** which is a search engine of search engines. It is wild!

If you are concerned about posting your résumé on the Internet or with a posting company, use your e-mail address only, rather than your full address as found on your professional résumé. Everyone can access the postings and the Internet ASCII files.

When you copy your résumé into an ASCII file, be sure that you use a keyword stripe. This is a list of industry and education buzzwords up to 65 characters in a line. It is placed at the left margin above your name. Separate each entry with a forward slash (/) as you place them on the line, for example:

BS/Acc't/3yrs mgmt exp/tax analysis/Novell certificate/real estate license

This is one place where acronyms and commonly used industry abbreviations are accepted. The optical character recognition (OCR) software that reads this ASCII version of your résumé will file the résumé in each of the six places indicated by your buzzwords. The future is already here. Companies have access to candidates with advertising in economies of scale, with management efficiencies, and have immediate access to qualified and technical pools of professional candidates.

Presentation Software

There is a wide variety of résumé software packages on the market. Some are available by downloading from the Net. The important thing to remember when selecting these software packages is that you want to know what they will assist you to do. Read and ask questions before purchasing. Several packages are listed at the end of the chapter, but you need to know all the facts in order to make an intelligent decision about what to purchase. There's a lot of junk on the market, too.

The best all-purpose software package I have seen on the market is Individual Software's ResumeMaker Deluxe CD. This software package provides help with designing and composing a professional résumé using step-by-step directions. It has a letter writer component so that a wide variety of cover letters can be quickly accessed and made to fit your needs.

There is a complete calendar and scheduler so that all your records can be kept in one place. This program includes a networking database so that you will not lose any of the contacts and information you want to retain for professional purposes after you have been hired. This is an excellent tool for those going into sales. This program includes an interactive interviewing process in which you can learn the dos and don'ts of interviewing and other tips about your performance in an actual interview. Other tools are suggested at the end of this chapter.

Continuing Research

These works continue the pattern previously established in earlier chapters.

Light reading, anyone?

Books

Christensen, Clayton M. *The Innovator's Dilemma: When New Technologies Cause Great Firms to Fail.* Cambridge: Harvard Business School Press. 1997.

Journals

Mardesich, Jodi. "If Business Cards Could Talk." *Fortune.* July 5, 1999. (*Fortune's* information technology special report)

Try these sites

General Web Site Search

www.about.com
   (Specific to college grads)

www.altavista.com
   (When you are searching a subject)

www.askjeeves.com
   (Any question will give you several options to consider.)

www.dogpile.com
   (A search engine of search engines, very helpful)

www.google.com
   (Search by keywords for best results.)

Résumé Research Web Sites

www.lycos.com/careers/careerguide/resume.html
   (Lycos Career Guide for Winners. Helpful feedback, searches, mail)

www.careermosaic.com/cm/rwc/rwc13.htn
   (Demonstrates how to change your Word résumé to ASCII text)

www.careermosaic.com/cm/rwc/rwc100.htn
   (Tips on using keywords for electronic résumés)

www.microsoft.com/pages/deskapps/word/is/default.html
   (Converts a Word document to HTML and can be downloaded free)

CD-ROM Business Card Web Sites

(These products are expensive, but very worthwhile for some.)

www.4thgear.com/Website8-30/cd_businesscards.htm

www.wfive.com/html/body_specifications.html

www.nichestuff.com/CD_Business_Card1.htm

www.crystalcanyon.com

Got a few extra bucks?

Software Programs

ResumeMaker Deluxe CD-ROM. Pleasanton, CA: Individual Software, Inc. 1999.
   www.mgendron@individualsoftware.com ($25.00)

Interviews Defined

Conversational interviews are the best part of interviewing for the potential employer and the candidate. In an interactive interview, both parties are treating each other as professionals in a field of common interest to each of them. Being able to continue a conversation with someone means you have listened to prior comments. Informational interviewing as well as job interviews require the candidate to have experience and skill at focusing comments and eliciting additional information at the same time.

Actual job interviews can be lengthy if the decision maker is interested in your credentials and personality. They can be numerous. I have had graduates tell me they were interviewed seven times before the decision makers got around to discussing options and allowing negotiations to proceed. Some graduates have been exposed to stress interviews. Others have experienced decision makers who want to hire them that day. There are pluses and minuses in each and all of these described scenarios for job interviews.

A completely technologically driven interview process is conducted over the Internet and requires a host of different skills, along with many of the traditional ones described in Chapter 5. Interviewing for a job these days takes background research preceding the interview, conversational skills to conduct an interactive interview, being prepared to answer and ask a continuing flow of questions so that both of you come away from a satisfying human experience while using the technology available to you.

Negotiation is a separate interview style and process. Most need to prepare for this process carefully and adequately because negotiation is the step from which you will move upward in the rest of your career. An application of *GAME theory* for the negotiation process is outlined and charted for the job searcher in Chapter 6. Sources for this adaptation include the works of John von Neumann and John Forbes Nash, Jr.; both were luminaries of Princeton University.

CHAPTER 4

Interviews

Interview Style

No one likes the twenty questions game that some interviewers use. It is demeaning to a professional and creates an appearance of needing to dominate the meeting mercilessly. Usually after an onslaught of these twenty questions that range from, "Tell me about yourself," to "What was the greatest failure you have experienced in your professional life in the last two years?", the candidate is worn out and has nothing to say to the interviewer when asked, "Is there anything you would like to ask me about the company or the job?" With a grateful heart that the end of this meeting has been signaled, the candidate responds, "No, I think I have a clear picture." Then the candidate leaves the scene of the accident.

Being able to maintain an interesting conversation is an art that is sadly disappearing from American culture. Pundits blame everything from dysfunctional family structures to poor education to cultural dissidence to "candidates aren't as good as they used to be." The trick for good communication in an interactive situation is to listen attentively to what has been going on in the conversation.

Examine a conversation where two people are enjoying each other's company. They are talking to each other, and each is interested in the other's comments and reactions to perceptions given. If one or the other is looking out the window, the attention expectation is broken. Either the topic is not of mutual interest, or one or both are not interested in having this conversation. Have you ever been with someone who came to a party or a dinner table with something to read? Besides just being rude, the offending behavior lets everyone else know that whatever you have to say is not in the least bit interesting.

On the other hand, two people can have a tremendously long conversation that lasts well into the evening because the interaction is great, no matter the topics. Let's examine why this is so. How can this interest be used to advantage in a job-related interview? One way to continue a conversation along the lines it has been proceeding is to ask an appropriate question after having made some comment or other. This questioning attitude engages the other party, and they maintain interest in keeping the conversation going. (See the movie *My Dinner with André*.)

An example dialogue between a decision maker and a candidate might follow this line.

DM "Glad you could make our meeting this morning. How can I help you?"

Cand. "As I indicated in my letter, I am interested in the position you have advertised in the *San Jose Mercury,* for a computer programmer. Is the position still open?"

DM "Yes, we hope to make a decision soon. What interested you about our ad?"

Cand. "The ad suggested that you were opening a new position of computer programmer due to your needs to upgrade your current software and initialize some new options for your sales force. That interests me very much, having been in sales the past three years while going to school. What does the job description say about your needs for this position?"

DM "We are still working on defining exactly what we want an employee in this position to do in our company, so we hope to find someone who would be looking for this type of open-ended position and ultimately would contribute to the definition of the job description. Are you willing to take that kind of a risk?"

Cand. "I consider myself somewhat of a risk taker, but I would need more definition than we have already discussed. Do you expect this programmer to be knowledgeable of managerial functions or programming functions in order to assist you in writing your organization's job description?"

DM "I think the managerial responsibilities are covered quite adequately, but we need someone with a contemporary background and education to fill in the places where we do not have the technical expertise. Is this becoming more clear to you what we are looking to hire?"

Cand. "Yes, but I would like to have the position clearly described before I would accept it. I would be willing to help define the job accurately, identifying exactly just what the position skills would entail with your managers. Are my expectations within your developing outline for the new position?"

As you can see, this is a back-and-forth conversation. Each one answers the question of the other and follows with a question that moves the clarification along. This candidate wants to help clarify the position but does not want full responsibility for writing the position description. The candidate also wants to have the description settled before considering it as an option for employment. Questions such as Where did you last work? (read the résumé), How long have you gone to school? (read the résumé), and Where do you want to be in 5 years? (who can predict the next week let alone 5 years from now?) are fillers that do not get to the substance.

Interview Manners

Interviewers are not all trained to do their job very well. Some may interact better than others do because their social skills are better developed. At the very least, you should be able to conduct an interactive conversation and encourage more equal participation with the interviewer. If the individual totally balks at this and forces you into the twenty questions game, then you know something about this company, and while you are most courteous, you leave at the best moment and continue your quest elsewhere.

This kind of conversational interviewing takes practice, so notice when you are with a good conversationalist how they behave, how they formulate their interaction to encourage reaction from others; notice their timing, their inferences, and facial expressions. Communication takes skill and practice to become perfect.

Interviewers are not all trained to do their job very well. Some may interact better than others do because their social skills are better developed.

If there are some traditional questions that you will be asked because of your industry, carefully script your answers, rehearse them before a mirror, and burn them into your memory. You do not want to sound like a robot when you answer, and yet your answer must be sophisticated and complete. You want to move on as quickly as possible to more meaty matters from your perspective. This will help you do that and move past a spot you do not want to cover any more deeply than you are prepared to do.

Many job searchers experience stress interviews. This occurs in companies which have a tradition of hassling or hazing prospective candidates to see if there is a weak spot. It can also be used in a company that has little time to interview adequately and needs to make job decisions quickly.

As a candidate you will not know which is the case, or it may be an arrangement somewhere in between these two points on a continuum. Just be prepared to answer, in a conversational style, the questions asked. If the interviewers have not introduced themselves (a breach of etiquette on their part), ask them if they would please identify themselves and the departments they represent within the organization. This type of interviewing can be intimidating, so it behooves the candidate to know as much about the people interviewing as can be known without appearing rude or hostile.

The scenario is usually a single candidate facing a bank of managerial types, each with a different department or discipline to cover responsibly. As indicated previously, answer each question straightforwardly and close with a question of the interviewer or someone else at the table. This encourages conversation between you and individual members of the committee. It may also precipitate a conversation among members on the committee, which will give you some insight into their management style and possibly provide information you would never get with a single interviewer. This is a minefield, but you can work it to your advantage. Keep in focus and do not allow them to change your focus, interest, or professional goal in talking with them.

Informational interviews are just that—conversations for more information than you already have discovered about a company or job responsibilities within a discipline or a job title. Remember that companies give job descriptions their job titles. The job title means only what the organization says it means. There are no universal job titles. That is why you need to understand the job

Informational interviews are just that—conversations for more information than you already have discovered about a company or job responsibilities within a discipline or a job title.

description in all its detail, rather than think you know what the job title means. There are chief of staff positions in the military, in banks, in political campaigns for people or issues, and in the White House. All carry the same job title, but the job descriptions vary widely.

There are many reasons why the wrong people get hired for a company or the right person ends up in the wrong job. Take your time. Finding the best job for your education, skills, and experience is hard work and consumes lots of time and energy. In today's market allow about 30 days of search for every $15,000 of salary you hope to command. This is a guideline, not a rule. Make sure the job description fits you, or you will be looking again soon. If the company you love doesn't do what you want to do, why go there for interviews? Your intuition is great, but also engage your brain in making these decisions about where you want to interview.

Interview Process

The interview process has several stages. First comes preparation. This means company research to determine what they want and how you can meet their goals effectively. Always be professionally prepared for the job interview—looks, résumé, interview style, courtesy, conversational style, arrive early, and review the questions you want to have answered by the time you come out of the building. Etiquette is imperative with all the people you meet on your way to and from the interview.

Second are the introductions. These are the bread and butter of communication, and they are so poorly delivered in most cases. Smile: it will gain you friends. Have a firm handshake, but not a bone crusher. Good eye contact says you look honest and sincere. Start the conversation with a cheery greeting and a professional manner. Bring your questions with you, but do not have them written on paper. That is why you have a brain. If something is important to you, you will remember what you want to ask.

Third, develop a conversational style of communication. Follow the information earlier described. If you don't understand the question, ask the interviewer to explain or clarify so you can give a focused answer. If you don't know the answer, say so and tell the interviewer you will look it up when you return to your office or home. Inform the interviewer you will return the answer to them when you have found it. And do so. By the end of the interview, be sure you have everyone's name and position title mentally stored so you can write appropriate thank-you notes to all you met.

During the interview, illustrate how your skills, education, and experience match a need that has been identified during the exchange. You know all about you, and the interviewer knows all about the company's goals and problems. The goal in your interchange is for the interviewer to find someone to assist with processes or problem solving within the company. Your goal is to find the best possible place to begin your career after graduation. Close every interview with a statement of your continuing interest in the company and the position discussed, if you are still interested. If you are not interested in the particular position discussed, say that and then elicit the help of the interviewer about where you might look to find exactly what you want in a position. Some will be extremely helpful, others will not. This level of help is available, but you do need to ask for it.

Interview Inhibitors

The physical manifestations of nervousness that need to be tamed include unconscious behaviors. In order to know what they are, record a mock interview and then look at it critically. Things that usually annoy others include leaning out of the chair or resting on the table, finger tapping, lip biting, toying with jewelry, frowning, adjusting hair or clothes, head wagging, hands covering or rubbing the face, chewing gum or cough drops, drinking, and smoking. This is true even if you are offered candy, gum, a drink, or the opportunity to smoke. These behaviors will detract from your decorum and could raise questions about your character, depending on how the interviewer views smoking and drinking. Remember you are always "on" for the interview.

Learn to maximize your facial expressions and body language to your advantage. Do not talk deadpan unless you are playing poker. If you have a constant smirk, get rid of it. If you tighten your jaw when you are nervous, be aware of it and conquer it. Don't cover your mouth when you talk. Do not cross your arms. Relax and be yourself.

The value of eye contact is so important. It communicates that you are prepared for this meeting. Good eye contact establishes a bond between you and the interviewer. This usually takes about 5 seconds, so don't stare. Staring makes people feel uncomfortable. Insert some humor into your decorum, but be careful. Keep in mind the sensitivities of your interviewer. It is possible you may be perceived as arrogant rather than humorous, and there go your chances for success in this company.

Take the time to dress appropriately for the interview. Interviewing is a managerial function, even though the job itself may be hanging cable between walls and buildings. Any jewelry needs to be expensive and preferably gold. Wear nothing that dangles or makes noise. Do not wear costume jewelry. Reduce the heavy makeup; you look like you are hiding something. No heavy cologne, perfume, or aftershave lotion is to be worn at all. Some people are actually allergic to the scent.

Wear clothes that fit you. If you have lost or gained weight, take a trip to the tailor and have your clothes altered accordingly. Shine your shoes and have them heeled if they need it. Match the various components of your outfit. If you cannot determine what looks good together, ask someone who can assist you. Wear a conservative-style suit, clothes, shoes, ties, blouses, shirts; you can always relax after you are hired. The way you look is often interpreted as the person you are.

Body language says a mouthful about you. It's not fair, but if you slouch and droop over when you sit, stand, or walk, the interviewer may interpret that you are lazy. If you have quick movements or make harsh sounds when walking on tile floors, you may be perceived as impatient, intolerant, or militaristic.

When you open your mouth to speak, be sure you can speak with the best language skills, as a professional would be expected to do. If you cannot do this, it will become painfully apparent very shortly. Communication comes out again and again in company surveys as the number-one deficit among young people right out of college. It seems as though our graduates are not prepared, with all their schooling, to speak and write in their native tongue very well. This is always perceived as a terrible problem, and some interviewers will not allow you an appointment if your résumé has an error on it or your telephone manner is not up to speed when you call for an interview. Keep religion and politics out of the conversation, unless those are the fields in which you are interviewing.

Stop and watch how professional people you respect dress, move, speak, interact with others, introduce people to one another, maintain eye contact, the level of voice they use, jewelry they do and don't wear, handshakes, smiles, and humor injected into their communication styles. You can learn a lot by watching successful people because you will need to be able to perform the way they do so well. With respect to speaking and writing, hit the books again or hire a coach. This is not molecular science. Everyone should be able to communicate well when all the words they have read, heard, and used are in one language. No excuses will be accepted.

Interview Types

PHONE INTERVIEWS

These are the most dangerous to handle because neither party can see the other to judge the communication signals that we all send. However, in today's fast-paced job search, candidates often make the mistake of accepting the job without having seen the company or talked with someone face to face. E-mail, fax, and voice mail are all technical tools with which we can interview. Encourage the interviewing company to arrange for you to meet them personally, if at all possible. Otherwise, you are flying up a blind alley. Look in a mirror while talking on the phone, and smile: it makes your voice sound more pleasant.

BEHAVIORAL INTERVIEWING

This is another style of interviewing used by some companies today. This style of interviewing is based on the theory that past behavior is predictive of future success. The questions are about skills, character, and preferences based on examples from your past work or school experience. This way the candidate is rated on past actions, not the gut reactions or intuition of the interviewer.

In traditional questions, the candidates may be asked what they think of overtime practices. In the behavioral mode, they would be asked to describe a time when they needed to work extra hours to meet a deadline or complete a task. The key idea in behavioral interviewing is to paint a picture of the thinking that underlies the decision making or the behavior without having to deal with unessential details. Though it is considered passé today, some may still use this type of interviewing, so be prepared. The approach today is toward a more sophisticated style of interviewing.

CONVERSATIONAL INTERVIEWS

As described earlier in this chapter, conversational interviews are preferred in today's marketplace. The reasons interviewers like this style is it leads to more candid responses, less memorized answers, and honest and forthright responses are more forthcoming from the candidates. The wrong interpretation one could take from this conversational style is to become too relaxed. In all interviews, even if the interviewer seems very nonchalant, remain professional, friendly, and cool.

COMPETENCY-BASED INTERVIEWS

This type of interview is growing in numbers among technical and managerial job interviews. This is a scientific approach that is based on the theory that the single-best predictor of future behavior is a person's recent past behavior. This usually means that given similar environmental experiences of a workplace, people tend to behave in a consistent manner. The first step defines specific competencies needed for a job—the job description set up by the organization. Second, the interviewer ascertains a candidate's respective level of skills in these necessary competencies. Third, the candidate who best meets these established competencies is offered the opportunity to negotiate the terms of the employment offer with the company representative or manager. The questions themselves are scientifically based in psychological theory. They are open ended and encourage the candidate to communicate their history more readily.

TEAM INTERVIEWS

Referred to earlier as stress interviews, they are usually an effort on the part of a company to get a variety of perspectives on job candidates. Usually many people may interview you at one time, maybe in a roundtable fashion, and then recommend their individual positions on hiring or not hiring you to the manager in charge. This can be in a formal setting, at a luncheon, or at a staff meeting, which the candidate may be permitted to observe. The trick here is that all the interviewers bring a wide variety of interviewing skills to the meeting, and there is no one person's style that is preferred.

Team interviews can be taxing, hence the use of *stress interviewing*, as the perspective of a job searcher. Be respectful and professional with each one you meet, because any one may cast a negative deciding vote. There may be a majority vote; the manager may make the decision but ask for input from other staff members. The team itself may make a collegial decision about a new member. You will not know how this is accomplished, so be professional at all times with everyone.

Conducting yourself professionally means to be friendly to everyone. Secretaries are often vocal about their reactions to candidates they have met. They see you first. A firm handshake in American business society is imperative. We usually smile and make eye contact at the same time. Look alert and professionally dressed. Watch your posture. Always send a thank-you note within 24 hours of the meeting to all who attended the meeting. A note to the secretary is a nice touch, and it will be noticed.

Sometimes we make bad mistakes. Oops! If you find yourself in a slipup, make amends early. If you have forgotten a colleague's name or address them by another's name, simple apologies are sufficient then continue whatever you were doing before the gaffe. Do not let private comments go beyond the hearing audience you intend. Criticizing others is almost always uncalled for, and frequently we are using inaccurate information. Have your facts and criticize only when it is absolutely necessary.

Do you overreact in awkward situations? Your reactions can be very telling to others. How would you react to suddenly catching your garment on a piece of furniture and tearing it? Did the boss see you kick the PC? If you make a clumsy error, apologize. Use profanity or off-color comments and jokes, and you will step into a lot of trouble. If this is your habit, undo it. You will eventually pay a heavy price. Others before you have learned the hard way. If you are observed talking to yourself, just comment something like, "Often the best conversation I have all day." Dropping things and tripping are things we all do, but when someone else is present, we feel silly. Humor helps a lot here.

In direct conversation, remember to watch your stance, maintain eye contact, and speak softly, clearly, and courteously.

Networking means talking to people you know and leading from them to others you don't know. The old saying, "It's not what you know, but who you know" is still true. The goal is to expand whom it is you know in the field of your choice. There are job-searching clubs of all sizes and dimensions. Professional associations usually provide this service, and alumni groups have a built-in resource for contacts.

Company Web pages often communicate their history, culture, products, and services they provide to the public, job listings within their walls, links to other inside information, business profiles, financial data, even addresses and phone numbers of executives, managers, and directors. Multiple company locations are also available from these sites.

The most important thing to remember is that etiquette rules apply everywhere. In direct conversation, remember to watch your stance, maintain eye contact, and speak softly, clearly, and courteously. On the Internet there is netiquette, which applies to the way you respond over the Net. Responding to e-mail follows the same etiquette rules as writing a letter. There is also chatiquette, which basically applies general business etiquette to chat rooms on the Internet. You still need good communication skills, such as correct English usage, accurate spelling, and precise punctuation, to communicate in chatiquette.

Interactive and conversational interviews are the norm today. The experienced and successful job candidate will excel in these types of interviews. However, there are some situations where the old rules still apply and the candidate must be prepared to act effectively in those situations as well. These skills are knowable. One can become more and more proficient with practice. Basically there is no excuse for poor interviewing on the part of the candidate. At least one of you should know what you are doing in order for the interview to be a successful one. That one is you!

Continuing Research

Light reading, anyone?

Books

Davidson, Alan D., Ph.D. *Competency-Based Interviewing*®: A Guide, 5/e. San Diego, CA: Davidson Consulting. 1999.

Journals

www.fastcompany.com

www.wired.com

www.workforceonline.com

Try these sites

General Web Sites

www.about.com
   (Specific information for college grads)

www.altavista.com
   (Information about specific topics)

www.dogpile.com
   (Search engine of search engines)

www.google.com
   (Search by keywords for best results)

Company Information Web Sites

www.hoovers.com
   (Information about company executives and financial info)

www.jacc.becon.org/national.htm

www.pri-teknet.com/services/resumesites.html

Job Interview Sites

www.careermosaic.com
   (One of the earliest and oldest job site collections; accents jobs west of the Mississippi)

www.monsterboard.com

(Counterpart to the Career Mosaic referred to earlier; accents jobs east of the Mississippi)

occ.com

(National coverage)

www.nationjob.com

(Emphasis on the Midwest)

www.4work.com

(Creates anonymous profiles that employers see)

www.americasemployers.com

(Keeps résumé posting active until you say otherwise)

www.espan.com

(Will post résumé for 6 months unless you update before that)

www.careerbuilder.com

(Focuses on needs of companies rather than job seekers)

www.jobdocnews.com

(Current research valuable to employers/employees today!)

Got a few extra bucks?

Software Programs

Davidson, Alan D. *SmartHire: Competency-Based Interviewing® for Windows.* San Diego, CA. 1995. **www.pcmusa.com** ($295.00—maybe not for you, but something you can share with the human resource people in your new company)

Job Interviews

Ads

Decoding ads today is a real art form. Here are some lines that may appear in a newspaper near you and an indication of how they could be interpreted.

"Join our fast-paced company." (We have no time to train you.)

"Casual work environment." (We don't pay enough for you to dress well.)

"Seeking candidates with a wide variety of experience." (Four people just got fired.)

"Problem-solving skills a must." (We are in chaos here.)

"Must be deadline oriented." (You will start 6 months behind schedule.)

"Must have good communication skills." (Management communicates; you listen.)

"Must be career minded." (Female applicants must be childless and remain that way.)

"Some overtime." (Some overtime each night and some overtime each weekend.)

"Requires team leadership skills." (You'll be a manager without pay or title.)

"No phone calls, please." (We have filled the position; incoming résumés are just a formality.)

These are funny analyses, but there is an element of truth in them. Bring any queries you have about the ad to the interview session. The company had something specific in mind when they phrased the ad in the manner you may be questioning. It may not be clear to you. It is up to the firm to clarify so that you will understand the position responsibilities in their entirety.

Often a graduate will complain, "How can I get work experience, if I can't get hired?" Graduates must bridge the gap from part-time or full-time but unchallenging work to full-time professional work in the field of their major. Today we enjoy the most welcoming hiring market we have experienced in years with regard to college graduates. Basically, graduates can settle into a field of their choice immediately upon graduation by working at it diligently.

Getting Started

Informational interviews allow the graduates to ask themselves, "Where would I like to work?" "In what kind of job will I make a contribution to the overall purpose of a company in my field?" "What kind of experience will I need?" Often a short-term job while going to school will yield long-term benefits upon graduation if it is related to your chosen field. Even volunteer work serves a good purpose if the graduate has built up a history of the needed skills for the new position.

Jobs are not gifts but trades between skills needed and compensation for use of those skills in line with a company need.

Graduates cannot assume that all they have to do is look out the door and say, "I went to school and graduated; now give me a job." Jobs are not gifts but trades between skills needed and compensation for use of those skills in line with a company need. Resist the urge to look at titles first. Companies define all job descriptions within their own job titles. No two companies use the same job description for the identical title. Ask about your responsibilities, chain of command reporting, and evaluation so you are clear about what the job title identifies.

It is a mistake to look at the salary only. Sharpen negotiation skills, and if you feel your skills are not going to be adequately compensated, prepare to move into the broader markets. Use the Internet and your own technical skills to find the wealth of jobs that are available. These opportunities keep growing day by day. Many managers have some back-burner projects they would love to have someone do. If that project or dream is in your field, but it only takes 20 hours a week, you may want to take it and then treat yourself as a consultant and look for other options of similar dimensions.

The best time to find these part-time options is while you are still going to school. Then the effects and skills of these opportunities will register favorably on your résumé. Once you find these kinds of jobs, perform in a stellar fashion so your references will be good when you are ready for a full-time professional job, having earned your degree.

It is rather easy for graduates to identify skills they have and the background for working with these skills in an industry of choice. The clearest mirror of your potential success is how you meet the challenge of your work habits. These include interpersonal communication, desire, enthusiasm, drive, attitude, discipline, and sensitivity. You will be hired for your accumulated skills, education, and experience. You will remain employed if you have the soft skills represented in work habits. These habits reflect your personality and cannot be changed very readily. Quite often the brightest and smartest do not make it in the world of working with others. Why is this? Among those who fail, it almost always has to do with their lack of soft skills.

Companies hire you for your revealed personality because they know they can train you to do things their way. What they cannot change is your attitude. So it is important that you understand the company culture of the group you are considering as your employment option. What you know changes, but who you are usually does not. If you ignore finding out the culture of a company, you neglect this at your own peril.

If you think you cannot find what you are looking for, then I would suggest that you try to broaden your search. Look on the Internet. Maximize your search to cover all options. Organize yourself so you can take advantage of the best options. Walking down the aisle to "Pomp and Circumstance" is only the beginning.

Who Are These People?

The best way to evaluate a company is to observe them. That is why it is so important to go to the place where you are planning to work and check out the environment. Talk with past and present employees. Ask the hiring manager for a list of recommendations about what previous workers thought about working for the firm. This is not arrogant, but can be asked arrogantly. Be careful.

Go to the company's Web site and discover what it says about the company. Then research with a search engine and find out what others think about the firm. The company has competitors, enemies, customers, former employees, and suppliers; maybe the company is a litigant. In some industries researchers monitor business practices. Read what these researchers have to say about the company you want to hire you.

No manager can hire someone who does not apply. So get before the hiring manager and sell yourself. This means know yourself. Then you will do a good job of selling yourself. Interviewing is a conversation between two professionals interested in the same work. You may be a beginner, but you do have some passion about the industry. Otherwise, why have you spent so much time, energy, and money pursuing knowledge of the field?

Be Prepared

What kind of people are companies looking to hire? Employers like people who give straight answers to questions. They are looking for people who can talk about their past experiences with reference to future expectations. Upon graduation you do not separate from your past. You bring all of your past life experiences with you to the next position you accept. What an interviewer wants to hear from you is a coherent story about your life. Try to couch your language in such a way as to reveal your character. You are a person accepting a job, not a degree looking for a place to hang on a wall.

You will be asked why you took a certain course within your job history. Know why, and communicate the answer intelligently. Prepare yourself for these interviews, and keep your eye on your goal. You want the best job possible. The interviewer wants the best possible worker. You are both looking for quality in your choices. Even what may look like a short fuse in quick telling, may reveal a character strength of honesty and hard work. It depends on how you tell the story.

The interviewer is interested in your stories and how you communicate them. The statistics are listed on your résumé. The interviewer may hire you, but not in spite of your résumé. You must manifest some human characteristics, such as soft skills, when you describe what it is you have done in the past in other situations. One of the reasons companies insist on multiple interviews is that few people reveal who they are in a 45-minute setting.

Today's companies usually work in teams with most of their projects and customer requests. Whether you are a team player or not is a big decision point in hiring. If you are a loner and want to work alone, then they will probably go past you to the next interviewee. Sometimes loners are perceived as difficult to work with by managers and colleagues. An emphasis on teamwork and personal flexibility will go a long way in today's job markets. One concept that most mangers express is that they want a winner, not a whiner.

An emphasis on teamwork and personal flexibility will go a long way in today's job markets.

Companies want to hire good people. Be one of those. This means that you have good people skills. Companies assume you have a level of technical skills or required skills after reading your résumé. After all, you did graduate from college. Being able to communicate clearly and well is an enormous asset in today's companies. The ability to zoom in and zoom out of a situation or project for vision and comparisons is a real asset today. Some people have only tunnel vision and find it very difficult to work in today's busy and sometimes hectic workplaces. They cannot see or think out of the box.

Then there is the matter of moving up within a company where you may be currently working. Be sure you have understood the process from the human resources (HR) office. Do not rely on hearsay here. The HR manager should be able to give you the details about skills needed and education or certification required for all potential open positions. Applicants have a right to know what the criteria for selection are. If an applicant must be a relative of the owner, that may limit your opportunities significantly.

As an employee candidate for an open position, you should be permitted to take all competency tests, establish credentials, and interview with the decision maker, as any outside candidate would do. If you are told that a strong candidate has already been selected, you can trust that assessment. When the choice is made, you also have a right to know why you did not make the cut. If it is a well-run HR department, that would be standard procedure.

If you interview for an in-house position, keep track of scores of the tests you took. File the report from the HR director about why you were not selected for the position. Make note if you need to earn another degree or certification in order to be seriously considered for any other similar position. This way you will be better prepared for the next opening that becomes available. Most candidates can accept losing if they have some assurance that the hiring process is fair.

Executive Recruiters

Being hotly pursued by a head-hunting firm can be very gratifying to your ego, but it can also take you down some blind alleys. You may lose valuable time in a hotly contested marketplace. It is your job to interview the recruiter if you wish to hire one to assist you with your search. It is important that you have certain knowledge about the background of the company and the individual advisor who will work with you.

When hiring an executive recruiter, make sure your needs are clear. You want this individual or this firm to help you market yourself in specific industries. If you have put together a good résumé, there is no need to change it unless you are convinced that you are going in the wrong direction for your next career position. If the firm makes use of the Internet, be sure you know where they are posting your résumé. Sign a contract or its equivalent, which allows them to post your résumé on the Internet or other Web sites. There are innumerable reasons why someone would not want a résumé posted so publicly. Consult with your advisor in the firm.

Electronic Interviews

HR people are advised against using electronic bulletin boards for finding new applicants. You can find the information you need by doing research yourself with all the search engines that are available. Do so. Get connected to newsgroups. They are not used for information sharing as much as for recruiting efforts. Chat rooms are OK. The technology is awkward right now, but it may improve in the future. For this reason, chat rooms consume a lot of time without much benefit to the searcher.

Listservs are a great tool for immediate feedback. You can come and go at will. Listservs work like the old bulletin boards used to except instead of notes and comments being stored at a central location, the information is distributed directly to the listserv membership via e-mail. Usually there is no charge for this service to the on-line participant. The downside is that you may be flooded with messages. These listservs can also be used to solicit information and advice. It is common to receive 30 to 45 messages a day once you have requested information from a listserv's groups. The more listservs you subscribe to, the more your responses add up to good options.

Both bulletin boards and listservs can be fonts of misinformation. They are best used for networking, benchmarking, and other research practices to get a variety of data. If you want salary guides or aspects of the law explained, look elsewhere on the Net.

In all things on the Net, you reveal more about yourself than you intend if you do not form the habit of reading your messages carefully before you send them. Send the message to yourself, and carefully read the monitor for corrections you may need to make. What you see is what the reader will see. Copyright rules and laws against slander apply in cyberspace. You are legally responsible for the messages you send.

Job Description

The job description is information you need to discuss with a manager before you accept a position. Prepare a series of questions about the job description for the next interview you have with the hiring manager. Be sure that the description clarifies the skills you will need to succeed in the position. It would not be untoward to ask why the position is vacant. If the prior person has been promoted, then you know this is a position from which people can step to another. If the last 6 months have had five people in the job, then you might want to pass on this one. There's trouble here, and you want a job with a future and greater security.

Feel free to ask the manager about the management style of the department in which the vacancy is. Listen carefully as the manager describes the way things are done in this firm. Whatever you do, remember to be enthusiastic and express interest until you are absolutely certain you do not want this job. Then be gracious and express your professional rationale for not wanting to interview further. Leave as gracefully as you came into the office.

Feel free to ask the manager about the management style of the department in which the vacancy is.

Finding the job of your dreams is not a matter of luck, as some would have you believe. Be conscious of that and continue to keep your eyes focused on the goal. Communicate your strengths and skills whenever you have a chance. When questioned about past experiences, that means people with whom you have worked, challenges you have successfully answered, projects you have completed, promotions you have earned, and skills you have strengthened and acquired. Problem solving is something every company does, and if you have been successful with this skill in the past, prepare to talk about it with enthusiasm. Maximizing options for improved operations is a skill that most companies want. If you have done this well, then speak up about these experiences. They are yours and only you know what it took to turn these experiences into successes. Speak your truth with passion.

Job interviews by themselves can be intimidating for the unprepared; they are a challenge for those who have done their homework. You can never be too prepared. Distinguish job interviews from informational interviews, understanding that informational interviews may lead to job interviews. Informational interviews that may lead to job interviews are those secured from career fairs, conventions, the exhibitors' personnel, chance encounters with someone with a pet project that you are prepared to handle, and short-term jobs that may become the base of your future consultant opportunities. Be alert to the electronic interviews and the skills you will need to take the best advantage of these options. There is great diversity in methodologies, technologies, and technical skills required to conduct electronic interviews that can lead the candidates anywhere. Be prepared!

Continuing Research

Light reading, anyone?

Books

Johnson, Spencer. *Who Moved My Cheese?: An Amazing Way to Deal with Change in Your Work and Life.* New York: Putnam/Dimensions. 1998.

Journals

Fisher, Annie. "Ask Annie" (monthly advice column about jobs), *Fortune.*

Try these sites

Business and Financial News Sites

www.dowjones.com

Company Information Web Sites

www.hoovers.com

www.jacc.becon.org/national.htm

www.pri-teknet.com/services/resumesites.html

www.hr-esource.com

(Great listserv reference for companies and practices within the human resources discipline. You may want to have a heads-up regarding practices and companies that show up daily on this Web site.)

<listserv@cornell.edu>

Job Interview Sites

www.careermosaic.com

(One of the earliest and oldest job site collections; accents jobs west of the Mississippi)

www.monsterboard.com

(Counterpart to the Career Mosaic referred to earlier; accents jobs east of the Mississippi)

occ.com

(National coverage)

www.nationjob.com

(Emphasis on the Midwest)

www.4work.com

(Creates anonymous profiles that employers see)

www.americasemployers.com

(Keeps résumé posting active until you say otherwise)

www.espan.com

(Will post your résumé for 6 months unless you update before that)

www.careerbuilder.com

(Focuses on needs of companies rather than job seekers)

CHAPTER 6

Negotiation

Preparation and persistence will win the day in negotiation of successful deals. If deal means something negative to you, then insert compensation for the purposes of this book. Negotiation is not war, and you should not attempt negotiation as if you will never meet this person or work for this company again in your career. Negotiation is an art and a science. The art is expressed with your sensitivity and soft skills. The science is having the numbers correct and understanding their relationship to one another in the total package.

Win–Win

Whenever possible—for our purposes all the time—make sure that in the negotiation you are trading benefits, money, time, and energy with some equanimity with the other party. Negotiation has a bad name because some people have not practiced negotiation carefully and sensitively over the years. The worst ones make the newspapers, and the next worse make the gossip rounds.

If you are negotiating terms, make sure you have allowed for the company negotiator to win some points whenever you win what you want. When you are very emotionally involved with the outcome, negotiation can become a big hassle. Some job searchers have intellectually accepted all the fears others' mistakes have trumpeted, others who may not have properly prepared for the interview may be justifiably afraid, or some are willing to accept the package deal. The company package is a one-size-fits-all arrangement. This maxim doesn't work with clothes, shoes, screwdrivers, wrenches, or anything else, so why would it work in this case when there is so much to negotiate?

GAME Theory

John von Neumann, one of Princeton's greatest luminaries, was fascinated with the study of games and how to devise winning strategies. John Forbes Nash, Jr., a Nobel Prize winner in economics, 1994, was intrigued with von Neumann's research and moved the research to more sophisticated levels. In this text, negotiation is treated as a serious game with winners and consequences.

Negotiation has a game format. Two sides are trying to win, but it is possible for each side to win. Both parties know the facts. The candidate has asked enough questions to satisfy whatever was not clear or not understood about the company policies and practices. Candidates should ask for and remember the rationale stated for these same policies and practices. The company is trying to discern what skills, education, talent, and experiences this candidate brings to the open position, as well as ultimately to other positions within the company over time. This can be a win–win situation if strategized correctly.

Negotiation has a game format. Two sides are trying to win, but it is possible for each side to win.

Negotiation Process

Negotiation is a process, not an event. You must be prepared. Know what the rules are in the company with which you are negotiating. Ask about the priorities, the rationale for their practices, the extension of their regulations, and whatever "why" and "how" questions you can come up with so your own preparation will be adequate. Companies have policies about money budgeted for positions. They have procedures about progression through the company to other positions. They know how their system works. You have to research and ask until you at least understand what is possible, that is, what the outside limitations are for each negotiable item.

Once you are satisfied you have all the responses to your questions, you are ready to begin preparation. You now understand the following:

■ rationale for the way things are

- priorities in the department
- salary limits and how they are set
- policy guidelines for department hiring procedures
- promotion factors that could improve your position
- education/tuition options if you continue to improve your skills with this company
- time off: vacation, personal leave, sick leave, holidays, funerals, jury duty, parental leave, family medical leave, religious celebration days
- insurance choices: menu offerings, multiple company options, ratio of premium payments, benefit ratios, workers' compensation
- indigenous options
- creative opportunities (you bring these to the negotiating table as exchanges or additions during the actual interview meetings. Have them prioritized in your mind. And have the rationale for your request on the tip of your tongue.)

Compare what you know and what you want and devise a negotiation strategy (see Figures 6.1 and 6.2).

Negotiation strategy 1.   FIGURE 6.1

COMPANY RATIONALE	CANDIDATE NEED
Salary range ($30K–$40K) Rationale for highest figures Potential for 90-day review	Strategize to capture the highest or better salary options by using the policies as rationale for asking.

Benefits:
Insurance (90–10 ratio)
    Family or individual coverage
    Medical coverage: HMO, PPO
    Dental, vision coverage
	Many companies have a menu of insurance options. Select carefully.

Education ($5K cap per year)
    Covers tuition, lab fees, no books
    A, company pays; B, company splits costs with you;
    C, you pay
	Going to school, increasing certification, or earning advanced degrees, even an appropriate seminar, all advance your skills and value.

Vacation (2 weeks annually)
    Sick leave—2 days before requiring doctor's note,
    5 days to insurance.
    Personal leave—3 days
    Family sick leave—as needed
	Some time off can be taken throughout the year rather than all at once; usually an arrangement with the manager. Significant religious celebrations can be days off; negotiate them early.

Stock options—as available
401(k)—available to all after 6 months
Indigenous options: 25% discount on items purchased
Creative options:
    $1,000 credit card limitation to purchase needed
    supplies annually for job performance
    Defined and reserved sales territory
    Company car
    Spouse's career counseling
    Quarterly paid return home arrangements for
    international staff
	Anything is negotiable. Be creative.
	What do you need to do a better job?
	Child care and/or elder care, sign-on bonus
	What trailing spouse benefit works?
	Adoption/new baby parental leave
	Health club memberships
	Casual dress
	Competency-based pay scale
	Hot skill bonuses
	On-site medical/legal aid for staff

| FIGURE 6.2 | Evaluate your needs and wants against the process described in the scenario. |

Accounting graduate with *magna cum laude* record, who held the office of president of the student council in her senior year, is looking for a job to begin a new career. She hopes to succeed in this new position, prepare for a CPA exam, get married, and have a family within the next 5 years. She has made the decision that she would like to be a career woman that also has a family.

FACTORS	MONETARY VALUE	PERSONAL DECISION VALUE
Salary	$25,000–$33,000	75 percent
Tuition Reimbursement	Entire cap $5,000	15 percent
Medical Benefits Package	Best of it	5 percent
Immediate Vacation	(Two weeks without pay: a break after school and before assuming the job.)	5 percent

PROCESS

Salary	Scale Point	×	Decision Value	=	Weight	Tuition	Scale	×	Decision Value	=	Weight
$33,000	10		0.75		7.5	$5,000	10		0.15		1.5
$32,000	8		0.75		6.0	$4,000	8		0.15		1.2
$31,000	7		0.75		5.25	$3,000	6		0.15		0.9
$30,000	6		0.75		4.5	$2,000	4		0.15		0.6
$29,000	5		0.75		3.75	$1,000	2		0.15		0.3
$27,000	4		0.75		3.0						
$26,000	2		0.75		1.5						
$25,000	1		0.75		0.75						

Vacation	Scale Point	×	Decision Value	=	Weight	Medical Benefits	Scale Point	×	Decision Value	=	Weight
2 weeks	10		0.05		0.5	Best	10		0.05		0.5
1 week	5		0.05		0.25	Average	6		0.05		0.3
None	0		0.05		0	Poor	2		0.05		0.1

Applicant wants: 35,000, $5,000 educational cap,   best medical,   and 2 weeks off.
Decision value   7.5   +   1.5   +   0.5   +   0.5   =   10.0

NEGOTIATION SESSION 2

Company offers: $29,000, $2,500 educational cap,   best medical,   and no vacation.
Decision value   3.75   +   0.75   +   0.5   +   0   =   5.0

Applicant counters $35,000, $5,000 educational cap,   best medical,   and 2 weeks vacation.
Decision value   7.5   +   1.5   +   0.5   +   0.5   =   10.0

Company counters $31,000, $4,000 educational cap,   best medical,   and no vacation.
Decision value   5.25   +   1.2   +   0.5   +   0   =   6.95

Applicant counters, $32,000, $5,000 educational cap,   best medical,   and 2 weeks vacation.
Decision value   6.0   +   1.5   +   0.5   +   0.5   =   8.5

Company counters, $32,000, $5,000 educational cap,   best medical,   and 1 week vacation.
Decision value   6.0   +   1.5   +   0.5   +   0.25   =   8.25

Applicant agrees.

Consider the salary aspects, then develop your strategy further to take into consideration the potential value and need for benefits. The chart in Figure 6.3 illustrates some potential options that could be negotiated as benefits. No one company will have all the options. Notice the charted options under the headings of traditional, modern, and creative. All three categories will be associated with the kind of company culture and industry you have selected. Plan your benefits strategy accordingly. Always have strategic items that you would like to have but would be willing to trade if the company option would benefit you more than the benefit you are willing to exchange.

Figure 6.3 depicts a wide variety of options other than money that may be negotiated and in some cases, the items are more important than money. This is true, provided the money is adequate and appropriate to the situation and position. Be selective and always prioritize your options. Have them clearly arranged mentally so you can trade intelligently.

Company managers usually admire good negotiation skills in a new hire.

Company managers usually admire good negotiation skills in a new hire. They see negotiation ability as a set of skills ripe for continuing advancement and promotion to better positions where these skills can be used advantageously for the company. If a benefit listed on the charts is unknown to you, research it with a search engine like **www.altavista.com** or **www.askjeeves.com.**

Ask knowledgeable people if some of your requests would be available in a new company before you begin trading for them. Never try to create a benefit request you don't fully understand. In your own mind, have a variety of options you care least about to trade out of your request, which then shows your willingness to negotiate. Have some things to throw away. Play poker!

Now that you know what is being offered, its monetary value, and whatever limitations exist in policy, you need to look at who you are and what you have to trade. In Appendix D you will notice a quick method for measuring your job acceptance criteria against your potential value in the marketplace. Keep the range in mind that you figure using the charts in Appendix D. If you answer the questions honestly and accurately, you will have a good approximation of your worth. The information from Appendix D is for you alone, not for the company negotiator. These are your cards; hold them close to your vest. The decision maker for the company also has cards to play that you will not see.

This process looks deceptively simple on paper. Always have a variety of options in each category to be negotiated so that when you are trading, you begin at the bottom of your priority list to exchange items. Each category is negotiated separately. Once both parties have agreed to an item (salary, 90-day review, education, training, tuition reimbursement), the item cannot come up again unless both parties want to renegotiate the issue. Either party may wish to defer agreement on an item and put it on the back burner until something else is negotiated first. If both parties agree, it will remain unresolved until they agree to deal with it. When negotiating, each side will begin with their best hope for success and barter back and forth until an agreement is reached.

Now you are ready to negotiate. Study your strategy. Try not to panic. You are the only one in the room negotiating for you and your family. Take it slowly, item by item. Recall the company policy about the issues you are negotiating with them. This is a trade-off process, so be prepared to trade something in exchange for items you ask of the negotiator for the company. Keep in mind that what you are currently earning does not dictate what you will accept as compensation for the new position. The former is a fact, and the latter is your

FIGURE 6.3   Compensation table.

TRADITIONAL COMPENSATION	MODERN BENEFITS OPTIONS	CREATIVE BENEFITS TO NEGOTIATE
Salary Items	**Salary Items**	**Salary Items**
Base salary	Base salary	Base salary
Variable pay	Variable pay	Variable pay
Stock purchases	Performance bonus	Stock purchases
	Taxation of fringe benefits	Signing bonuses
Insurance Items	Golden parachute agreements	Short-term % increase in salaries
Health care insurance	Foreign earned income credits	Hot skill bonus
Accident/health plans	Partnership compensation	Aggressive IT merit increases
Group life insurance	Stock purchases	Early reviews/salary increases
Disability insurance options		Performance pay
Medical plan options	**Work/Life Balance**	Pay increases timing
Dental/vision plan options	Personal car for business	Direct deposit checking systems
Long-term/short-term disability insurance	Child and day care	Comp time for spent travel time
	Dependent care assistance	Paid airline memberships for travel
Retirement Options	Adoption assistance	Additional pay for weekend travel
Savings	Annual allowance for trailing spouse	Paid exercise fees while traveling
Stock plans as compensation	Home PC and Internet in remote location	Performance-based variable pay
Social Security	Contract agreements with spouse	Team incentives
Medicare/Medicaid	Club membership dues	Gainsharing/results sharing
Supplemental security income (SSI)	Per diem expenses	Broadbanding
IRAs	Mileage allowances	Skill-based pay
Profit sharing	HIPPA* compliance	Paid sabbaticals
Stock bonus plan (ESOP)	Matching gifts participation	Merit pay for stellar performances
Qualified employer retirement plans	Flexible hours	Early reviews/salary increases
Leveraged stock ownership plans	Company-paid business travel insurance	Part-time employee share benefits
Deferred compensation	PTO for military leave	Part-time PTO
Tax-deferred annuities	PTO for jury duty, bereavement	Part-time flexible scheduling
401(k)/403(b) plans	Paid dry cleaning for business travel	Part-time fringe benefits access
Pension plans	Alternate schedules	Part-time disability coverage
Stock purchase plans	Child-friendly atmosphere	
	Company family Christmas parties	**Relocation Costs**
Education	Reimbursement accounts	Intercultural training for family
Course work	Company family Easter egg rolls	Home search services
Certification	Flexible spending accounts	Roadside assistance
	Child care referral services	Family relocation counseling
Vacation Items	Health-wellness screenings	Quarterly paid return home arrange-
Vacation pay	Annual flu shots	ments for international workers
Time off	Stress reduction clinics	Language assistance
	Unique work environments	
	Family picnics/celebrations/ball games	

(continued)

*Health Insurance Profitability and Accountability Act of 1996

TRADITIONAL COMPENSATION	MODERN BENEFITS OPTIONS	CREATIVE BENEFITS TO NEGOTIATE
Other Benefits	**Career Maintenance Options**	**Work/Life Balance**
Relocation costs	Employee assistance programs	Hours/time leave banks
Employee vesting	International assignment assistance	Life partners beneficiaries of benefits
Public recognition	Career counseling	10% time/facilities for own projects
Career development	Professional development	Paid time off banks
Achievement awards	Mentoring programs	Technology for home workplace
Entertainment expenses	New employee referral bonus	Elder care
ERISA considerations	Team-building skills training	Trailing spouse options
Divorce and spousal rights	Problem-solving groups	Casual dress
Service awards	Redefining work competencies	Life/work sensibilities
Gifts of hams, turkeys, steaks	Domestic/foreign operations balance	Life/career cycles planning
	Employee empowerment practices	Prescription programs
	Paid school teaching/coaching	Flexible spending accounts
	Quality circles	Wellness/fitness programs
		Parental leave (birth/adoption events)
	Insurance Benefits	Geriatric care management/assessment
	Medical physicals/insurance	Healthy aging programs
	COBRA	Home care support
	Portability of insurance benefits	Nursing home ombudsman
	VEBA*	Transportation for elder care
	Cafeteria insurance plans	Massage therapy/nap time options
		JIT care in emergencies
		Summer child care options
	Retirement Options	Physical/mental impairment care
	Section 423 stock purchase plans	24-hour on-site meals/carryout
	Phantom stock plans	Monthly housecleaning services
	Junior stock	On-site medical/legal aid
	Savings plans	Accent concierge services
		New car negotiations assistance
	Time Off Items	Laundry services
	Sick leave/personal leave	$1,500 personal travel needs annually
	Family medical emergency leave	
	Religious holiday leave	**Career Development**
		Mentor/protégé relationships
	Child Care Options	CD-ROM business cards
	On-site care, backup care	JIT training as needed
	schoolage care, sick-child	Team incentives
	care, nonstandard hours care,	Diversity skills training
	paid family leave, resources &	Formal job skills training
	referrals, childcare discounts/	Outsourcing arrangements
	reimbursements, assistance for	
	students/trainees/low-wage	
	workers, children in the workplace	*(continued)*

*Voluntary Employees' Beneficiary Association 501(c)(9)

FIGURE 6.3   **Continued.**

MODERN BENEFITS OPTIONS	CREATIVE BENEFITS TO NEGOTIATE
Relocation Costs	**Retirement Options**
Double mortgage payments	Savings
Repairs on house to be sold	Stock plans as compensation
Contract with relocation services	Social Security
Help reduce college debts	Supplemental security income (SSI)
Life partners career services	IRAs
Temporary housing needs	Profit sharing
Trips between work and family	Stock bonus plan (ESOP)
Pay closing costs	Qualified employer retirement plans
Moving fees	Leveraged stock ownership plans
Reliable local homes market aid	Deferred compensation
Referrals to relocation-savvy companies	Tax-deferred annuities
Identify reliable mortgage lenders	401(k)/403(b) plans
Personalized counseling for	Pension plans
preapproved loans	Stock purchase plans
Traditional family relocation travel needs	Broad-based stock plan
Third-party relocation firms	
Job search employment help	**Other**
Ship belongings	Open book management practices
Finance house-hunting trips	$1,000 limited annual credit for supplies
Family transition support	Gamesmanship for all
Community familiarization trips	Paid child care at home for travelers
Pet relocation services	Paid elder care at home for travelers
Continuing elder care services	
School identification for family	
Multitiered formal relocation package	
Educate managers about relocation	
Area orientation services	
Backup child/elder care options	
Language assistance	
Assimilation assistance	

decision, arrived at with the company negotiator. Once you have prepared your strategy, summarize it and commit it to memory.

The name of the game is not money or salary but total compensation. Benefits are expenses to the company and a lucrative option for you and your family. Companies are willing to provide benefits for several reasons: (1) It helps them attract and retain top-grade talent, (2) benefits extended cover common personal and family needs that will affect the new employee, and (3) companies merit tax breaks on their profits for providing employee assistance options. The ratio of salary to benefits at the bottom

The name of the game is not money or salary but total compensation.

scale of total compensation value is 70 percent salary to 30 percent benefits. However, some benefits may raise the ratio as high as 60 percent to 40 percent. Now you are ready. Good luck!

The big day has arrived, and your are face-to-face with the company negotiator or manager. Learn to be comfortable with silence. The company negotiator may try to have you begin first. Should this happen, begin by summarizing what you understand the job to be, accent your responsibilities as you understand them, and indicate the job title, hours of working, and other job requirements (about 3 minutes should do). Do not raise the topic of money. That is the negotiator's role, and although you are ready to begin negotiating, let him or her open the negotiation.

Companies often start with a low offer. This can take the wind out of the candidate's sail. Don't let that happen. Counter with the strategy you put together before you came to the negotiation session. Do not be intimidated. With a clear understanding of their policies and practices, you can make a case for everything you want. You have set your limits before you began this session, so don't be hurried into changing your view, especially if you have strong backup positions based on their policies and stated rationale.

For example, if it is your opinion that you are worth more than the highest salary they are offering, back it up with comparable data about others in the industry who do the same work and have the same education. Use the requirements list for the position to demonstrate that you meet all of those requirements, and in addition you may have something else, such as Japanese-speaking proficiency or military experience in Europe. Do not state that you just want a better salary; you must indicate and justify why your requested salary is fair compensation for the talent, education, and skills you would bring to the company.

It also helps if you know the needs of the other side. This puts you in a strong negotiating position. If you know the organization may soon become a force in a European market, you may indicate you have military experience in the European theater, at the right time. Both you and the hiring manager know it is not a qualification for the current position, but it is something that could be needed later. He or she may decide you are more valuable than a candidate who just meets their qualifications list.

Listen to the other side. The negotiator is telling you something. If there is resistance to one of your requests, try to ascertain why your suggestion is opposed. An example would be that the company is insisting that you come to work the Monday after graduation, but you want to have at least 2 weeks off from your hard work during your graduating term.

There may be a client meeting scheduled with the team that is going to do the work, and you are on that team. Once you know this, you can negotiate permission to attend the meetings only and have nonmeeting days off until you officially begin work 2 weeks later. Arrange to be paid a consulting fee or some appropriate stipend for your time spent with your new colleagues and the firm's client.

This is where all your prior research pays off in big dividends. Remember that companies are looking for someone to fill an important need in their organization. Often they are trying to tell you how to make the best deal, so pay attention. You are there beginning a relationship with these people for whom you want to work. So begin on solid ground; be likable. There is such a thing as the power of nice.

You must always be prepared to walk away if you cannot get what is just and fair, no matter how skillfully you negotiate. Be sure you have thought of alternatives to this job before you go into the negotiation phase. That is why it is so important that you interview with at least 20 people a week. You will have other options to consider. All is not dependent on one negotiation effort. There is a difference between wanting a deal and needing a deal. You are negotiating more than money if you recall that everything is negotiable. Your preparation is key here. Perception is all. Usually neither side has all the cards, so play the game well.

> *You must always be prepared to walk away if you cannot get what is just and fair, no matter how skillfully you negotiate.*

Trade your concessions; never give them away. This is a *quid pro quo* situation, and it is your job to enable the manager to perceive that you understand this and are prepared to deal. In most cases, about 80 percent of the negotiation concessions will be made in the last 20 percent of the time allotted for this exercise. Be available to negotiate. Don't be aggressive or get into an argument with the other negotiator. Be prepared with a goodwill gesture that isn't costly to you. This offer usually surprises your adversary totally but is appreciated nonetheless. This ends the negotiation on a high note. Win or lose, do not criticize the opponent. Be your gracious self. You had planned to drop some of your requests in your preparation. Stick with the plan.

Continuing Research

Light reading, anyone?

Books

Fuld, Leonard. *The New Competitor Intelligence: The Corporate Resources for Finding, Analyzing, and Using Information about Your Competitors.* New York: John Wiley & Sons. 1995.

Kahaner, Larry. *Competitive Intelligence from Blacktop to Boardrooms—How Businesses Gather, Analyze, and Use Information to Succeed in the Global Marketplace.* New York: Simon & Schuster. 1996.

Nasar, Sylvia. *A Beautiful Mind: A Biography of John Forbes Nash, Jr., Winner of the Nobel Prize in Economics, 1994.* New York: Touchstone Books. 1999.

Shapiro, Ronald M., Mark A. Jankowski, and James Dale. *The Power of Nice: How to Negotiate So Everyone Wins—Especially You!* New York: John Wiley & Sons. 1998.

Steinberg, Leigh, and Michael D'Orso (Contributor). *Winning with Integrity: Getting What You're Worth Without Selling Your Soul.* New York: Random House. 1998.

von Neumann, John, et al. *Theory of Games and Economic Behavior.* Princeton, NJ: Princeton University Press. 1980.

Journals

Evans, Elaine M. and Susan Fabre. "A Total Rewards Approach to Compensation." *Solutions.* April 1999. Pages 31–35.

Imperato, Gina. "Land a Job Online." *Fast Company.* August 1998. Pages 193–198.

Joyce, Amy. "Career Track: True Confessions and Their Consequences." *Washington Post.* November 15, 1999. Page F09.

Madigan, Carol Orsag. "Friendly Persuasion." *Business Finance Career Guide.* September 1998. Pages 30–33.

Williams, Valerie and Jennifer E. Sunderland. "New Pay Programs Boost Retention." *Workforce.* May 1999. Pages 36–40.

Try these sites

Negotiation Information Sites

www.familiesandwork.org

www.hrwire.com

www.workforceonline.com

www.fanniemae.com

www.benefitslink.com

www.benefitnews.com

www.hire.com/candidates/sites.php3

www.prudential.com
(Highlight "Spotlight" for a copy of their ideas about employee benefits.)

Reports and Surveys

www.atlasvanlines.com
(Relocation survey)

www.cch.com
(Chambers of Commerce Clearing House)

www.doc.gov
(U.S. Department of Commerce)

www.fuld.com
(Competitive Intelligence Guide)

www.scip.org
(Society of Competitive Intelligence Professionals)

www.asaenet.org/index.html
(Gateway to Associations by the American Society of Association Executives)

www.hoovers.com
(Hoovers On-line)

www.pathfinder.com@7Q504wUAMvuS4bZ/business/text.html
(Pathfinder Money & Business Sites)

www.computerworld.com
(Salary and Satisfaction Survey—*Computer World*, annual publication)

www.shrm.org/issues/survey
(Wall Street Journal Compensation Poll)

www.manpower.com

www.us.deloitte.com
(Survey of human resources practices)

www.bls.gov/ebshome.htm
(Survey of the Bureau of Labor Statistics about benefits research)

www.homefair.com/homefair/cmr.salcalc.html
(Salary Calculator®)

www.us.kpmg.com/intlserv
(Survey covering the consequences of better pay for professional work in 1999)

www.jobdocnews.com
(Continuing research topics and tips for today's market)

Marketing

Marketing yourself and moving to new horizons combine individual effort with an identified goal and purpose. The fact that there are people with grade point averages of 4.0 who are walking the streets looking for jobs, while people with grade point averages of 2.9 are having success signing onto jobs has more to do with marketing than anything else. It is not the smartest candidate who gets the best job, but the best-marketed candidate who wins all the prizes.

Marketing is a process, as outlined in Chapter 7, and a potential, as described in Chapter 8. The candidate has a defined place to put the résumé. The résumé is the product promotion. The price is what the market will bear for accumulated skills, education, and experience. And the product is the candidate's accumulated talent finely honed for the markets of choice.

The market potential is worldwide today. Technology makes it possible for prepared candidates to sell their skills anywhere in the world. Their individual talent and skill will propel them forward. Creativity is supported by technology that enables the graduate's information to go anywhere—24 hours a day, 7 days a week. Even while the candidate sleeps, technology is making the résumé information available to whoever is looking for this defined talent.

Entrepreneurship is the hope and dream of a few of the graduates. This takes a specific kind of selling in order to succeed in a very tight marketplace. Preparation for business ownership requires the candidate makes sure these first forays into entrepreneurship have some support. This support can come from family knowledge of business ownership or from observing a small-business owner and taking on all of his or her odd jobs to get a real feel for what it means to own a business. The main thing that practitioners of this art need to remember about entrepreneurship is that when you are not open, your competitors are and they far outnumber you. If you like those odds, entrepreneurship may be for you.

The section closes with some thoughts in Chapter 10 about business politics. Candidates will be hired because their skills are current, their knowledge is recently minted, and their awareness is cutting edge, but in today's world that will all be tarnished in 6 months unless they can keep learning. As was indicated in Chapter 5 you will be hired for your skills and fired because you have little or no soft skills. Is that fair? No, but it happens.

Marketing has many faces: process, potential, entrepreneurship, and politics. Each requires the candidate to come forth and sell the talents, skills, education, and experience possessed. Good employees keep selling, constantly improving themselves with seminars, degrees, certifications, and active reading in their field. In other words, they do not grow stale in their knowledge of the field nor do they omit practicing the personality skills that keep them employed.

CHAPTER 7

Marketing Process

When one studies marketing in today's colleges, the first principle that is established is the marketing process. This process is communicated in a variety of ways with diagrams, outlines, and reams of prose. The main tenets are that in all marketing, four aspects are uppermost in the mind of the marketer. There must be (1) a product, (2) a determined price for the product, (3) promotion of the product, and (4) a place to distribute the product to the buyers. This is known in marketing literature as the four Ps.

The Four Ps of Marketing

Candidates for new jobs upon graduation are embarking on a marketing campaign. Candidates themselves, with all their skills, talent, education, and experience, are the *products*. The candidates are not for sale, but the use of their skills and education is. Having researched the market, the candidates can come up with a fairly accurate gauge of what a realistic salary range would be for that first job in a new career.

Promotional devices used to be a résumé and cover letter alone. Today there is technology that makes the résumé content visible in various formats, depending on the creativity and talent of the candidate or friend of the candidate. Distribution of the information about the candidate is in the hands of the candidate, and technology makes it extremely easy today to get your résumé before the eyes of a decision maker who might just be looking for you.

Look a little deeper. The product is the candidate with all the accumulated skills, education, certification, experience, and innate talent. The product is not the individual but the individual's accumulated treasure chest. As with any product, the candidate wants to look good, make a good impression, and entice an employer to hire the accumulated virtues and accomplishments of the graduate.

Therefore, the candidate must be in best form all the time. You never know when an opportunity will present itself for you to talk about your earned skills, job searching, completed education or certification, and work experiences. You have to be prepared to bring up the topic everywhere and sustain the interest of the listener, if only to describe the "product" in its best and most appealing form.

Whenever you are asked, "What do you do?" your answer should be "I am currently in a job search as I have recently graduated from _____. I am now prepared to work professionally in _____." If you have intrigued the listener with those two sentences, then you may be on your way to the interview

You are looking for the job of your dreams from the moment you enter your senior term.

of your dreams and the best job available. It is not magic. It requires hard work; the ability to meet strangers and friends with a straight eye and smile and tell them what you really are doing takes skill and sensitivity. You are looking for the job of your dreams from the moment you enter your senior term. Take advantage of the opportunities that fall your way while preparing the best marketing campaign you can put together.

Using the information outlined in Appendix D, you can reasonably arrive at the second P, a *price* for your skills and services. These charts will enable you to identify the soft skills that make job satisfaction possible and put on paper the facts about the compensation you need for these skills.

Then when that is clear to you, you are ready to do the second outline, which asks for comparison information about your dream jobs, compared against the market and coupled with your own earning history to date. Using this data and following the formula on the page, you will be able to calculate a fairly reasonable computation of salary range for you to consider in the market of your choice. You could make a lot of money as a national trial attorney, but only if you are educated and skilled at law. Comparisons are valid only among like things.

Promoting your résumé and its contents can be a 24/7 proposition. You cannot conduct a 24-hour-a-day, 7-day-a-week marketing campaign without the current technological advances to assist you. You cannot do global marketing of your skills and education without the assistance of the Internet and résumé posting firms. The costs are so reasonable compared to the opportunities you have available. While you sleep your information can be traveling all over the nation and the world, and when you wake there will be offers and interested employers seeking more information about you. Read the earlier chapters on résumés and their formats so you can take advantage of what technology can do for you.

Finally, you are in charge of *place*—where this information will be distributed. The range is far and wide. You select the Web sites, you design the résumé, and you post it on the Internet or with a posting firm. You send your professional résumé with a cover letter to decision makers of your choice. You take résumés to career fairs and distribute them to the firms of interest to you. There is no place you cannot reach with your résumé.

Marketing Campaign

For those who have created cyberspace résumés, do not send these to decision makers unsolicited. These résumés have to be received where the correct equipment can bring them to the monitor of the decision maker's personal computer. These are better hand carried and demonstrated on the spot. If you see that the equipment is not capable of receiving your résumé, inquire if the decision maker would like to see your résumé in HTML. A cyberspace résumé demonstrates your technological know-how to potential employers.

Marketers in career search firms talk a lot about the "hidden market." Approximately 75 percent of the job market is hidden. In order to reach that market, one has to make contact with decision makers in the career field or others who will take you to the decision makers.

By hidden market, we mean those jobs that are open, but only in-house personnel know about them. Some employers pay bonuses if the employees help recruit new people. Some decision makers have pet projects that they have not yet been able to implement, and then you arrive for an informational interview and they can see that you have the skills to take on their favorite project. You could be hired on the spot. Be careful. Jobs in the hidden markets are not deliberately kept from the public, but they have not yet been offered for the public's consideration. If you get there ahead of the public by informational interviewing, you may be the choice.

Designing a marketing campaign is essential to make use of all the assistance you need to get you and your résumé before the decision makers in your career field. From your campaign outline, you will be able to make weekly and daily plans that will enable you to arrive where you want to go. This process is not a matter of luck, but of hard work.

Marketing Workhorse Ps

Marketing workhorses are prospecting, profiling, and prioritizing. *Prospecting* means looking in all the expected places for the right companies and their respective managers or decision makers and looking for individuals who can help you get where you want to go. In old Westerns, we see prospectors looking for gold by a stream. There is gold in your prospecting, too. Keep at it and constantly look for the next set of opportunities.

Profiling means basic research. Who are these companies you have discovered? Who are these people who have been referred to you or you have discovered on the Internet, in a commercial, on television, or the radio? Once you know who they are and where they operate in the company and in the field, you are on your way to prioritizing.

Prioritizing means to compare and contrast in order to select the best order of people and companies that will serve your goals in the campaign. This requires judgment and careful soliciting of information, verifying the information you have, and then preparing a way to meet these people or get inside these companies to see what you might be able to offer them by way of your skills, education, and experience.

> *Prioritizing means to compare and contrast in order to select the best order of people and companies that will serve your goals in the campaign.*

Personal referrals are the best source of prospects. Whenever someone gives you a recommendation to a company, ask them if they know anyone in the company. Always secure permission to use the individual's name when identifying how you have this reference. If they do not let you use their name, then you will have to secure references from others into the company. This then becomes a prioritizing issue.

Figure 7.1 offers a visual representation of the marketing process as it relates to job searchers. Keep this diagram in mind as you flesh out your campaign into a market plan to be implemented as soon as possible.

Understanding the tools of marketing and putting them to use will enable candidates to locate the best possible positions available in the workplace of choice. These tools take a bit of time and energy to implement and use, but they pay off well in the end. In addition, good marketing skills will be an asset in your continuing career, especially if you enter sales and marketing.

FIGURE 7.1 **The marketing cycle.**

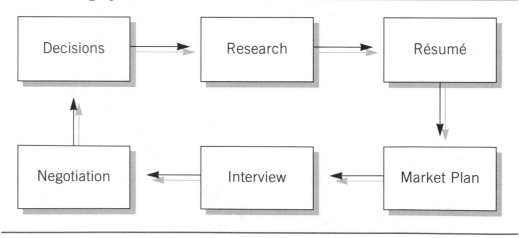

Continuing Research

Light reading, anyone?

Books

Burg, Bob. *Endless Referrals.* New York: McGraw-Hill. 1998

Leeds, Dorothy. *Powerspeak.* Berkeley: Berkeley Publishing Group. 1996.

Weylman, C. Richard. *Opening Closed Doors: Keys to Reach Hard-to-Reach People.* New York: Irwin Professional Publishing. 1994.

Try these sites

Marketing Research Links

www.salesprofessional.com

www.superwisdom.com

www.imarketinc.com

www.ceoexpress.com
 (Directory of links)

www.corporateinformation.com
 (Information about non-U.S. companies)

www.whowhere.com/Business
 (Locate specific persons)

www.clement.com

CHAPTER 8

Market Potential

The greatest potential for exposure in the marketplace of your choice is with today's technological resources. A well-designed market plan will have as a top priority the use of technology to make the candidate visible. Using e-mail and voice mail, on-line communications with company decision makers, understanding business trends in one's field, maximizing skills for education options and e-commerce, along with learning e-trade as current and future working tools will be imperative for the candidate who wants the best job possible in today's market.

One thing that is constant in today's work world is change. Nothing remains static and everything is in line for improvement, updating, downsizing, or uploading. Flexible persons who can manage this chaos in life will be in demand. New candidates for positions must know their subject areas and couple that knowledge with their street-smart awareness and wits. Market plans are a part of one's strategy to achieve the best possible position available.

Market Plan

Your market plan should contain the following in order to transcend the competition, which will be fierce:

- Identify your immediate career objective. (What do you want to do?)
- Estimate realistic support for achieving that objective (education, skills, experience).
- Develop résumé content.
- Design at least four résumé formats (professional, ASCII, posting firms, cyberspace options—PowerPoint, C++, Visual Basic, HTML).
- Arrange interviews to cover 100 percent of the market.
- Know who can help you reach your goal.
- Assess people's advice (realistic, unbiased, your interest counts, etc.).
- Evaluate leads before chasing every one of them.

This list is written as a map of how you would build a good marketing plan. To augment your plan, use market analysis techniques. These research materials are found in libraries, in company offices, and on the Internet. The better the research, the more prepared you will be for anything that may come your way in interviews with decision makers. Libraries have abstracts, program presentations, government briefs, academic condensations, professional synopses, scholarly monographs, and other ways to analyze the market in your industry. Internet sites are extremely current and accessible. Consider the list at the end of this chapter for references.

In your preparation and implementation of the market plan, consider all the people you meet on information and job interviews as customers. How would you treat a customer to whom you wanted to sell a product or a service?

- Return all phone calls as promptly as possible. (Don't give them a chance to call your competition.)
- Be courteous and respectful to all you meet. (Secretaries included.)
- Slightly underpromise what you can do. (Protects you against the unexpected.)
- Listen carefully. (You may have heard it before, but it can't be overemphasized.)
- Keep notes on what the decision makers say is important. (Summarize after the meeting.)
- Send thank-you notes within 24 hours. (This really makes a good impression.)
- Memorize the names of key interviewers, their positions, and keep expressing interest.
- Ask enough questions to know what they expect from you.
- Research and ask decision makers questions about company organization and company culture. (Only ask questions you could not have answered with your own research.)
- Follow the suggestions interviewers make as soon as you can. (Report back.)

The e-Words

E-mail is one of the fastest and most direct ways to reach someone in today's markets. Because of the speed with which these tools access information, one must be careful to check spelling and grammar. Technology may be the only way you can reach some decision makers. You never get a second chance to make a first impression, which are often lasting impressions. E-commerce is the way business is conducted on line today. The companies you are interviewing may have a cyberspace connection. Research it to prepare for your first interview.

Interviews may be conducted on line. Be prepared. Compose articulately and carefully when you answer any e-mail questions or participate in electronic interchanges.

Once you have started your plan, it is very difficult if you need to stop and fill in a blank you overlooked, hurriedly passed over, or deemed unimportant at the time of your investigative research and planning. No item is unimportant, no detail is too small to build a good marketing plan that fits your strategy. Market plans progress at an unfathomable speed, so do not be caught without one. Companies will continue to interview others while you go back and catch up with a résumé design flaw, a company history lesson, or any other missing piece of your preparation before you implement your market plan. If you don't take time to do it right the first time, you will have to take time to redo it, and that detracts from your readiness and potential.

Market plans progress at an unfathomable speed, so do not be caught without one.

VOICE MAIL

Some companies hire receptionists without training them about how the telephone is to be answered. When you call, they say the name so fast that you do not know what they said. Some are chewing gum or candy and cannot answer clearly. This is the first person the caller meets in a company. Some telephone etiquette is so bad that people do not call back again. Thus, voice mail systems may be a plus in some ways.

Learn to use voice mail. It is an important aspect of communication today. Often you will call and the tape is running. This can be frustrating, but try to think of it as an opportunity to express your best self. The tool is the telephone. First, if you are creating a voice mail tape for your own telephone to receive phone calls during your search, make sure the tape is error-free and your voice is pleasant. Speak slowly and do not do any "cute" things to distract your caller and impress on him or her the fact that you are not serious about this call. Remember, you are not making this tape for your friends and family, but for business purposes. This would be so even if you think Steven Spielberg or George Lucas will be calling to offer you a job.

Pronounce your name clearly and slowly. If you do not want to use your name, say, "Hello. You have reached 342-9087. I cannot take your call right now. Please say your name and send me a short message. I will call as soon as I am able. Thanks for calling." If you have a mirror in front of you while you make this tape, smile into the mirror—it will give a more pleasant sound to your voice.

When you call someone and must put a message on their voice mail, consider the following rules of telephone etiquette:

- Identify yourself. (In business we rarely identify people by their voices like we do in personal calls. Even if you have a distinctive voice, identify yourself.)
- Mention the reason for your call in as brief and comprehensive a way so as to enable the recipient to understand the purpose of your call.
- Don't rush your speech, don't garble your name, and if you give a telephone number, keep in mind that clarity is of the essence here.
- Spell your name for clarity.
- Suggest a time when you can be reached.
- Always repeat your phone number last.

Evaluating Interview Performance

How can you know an interview is going well, whether on the telephone, the Internet, or in a personal encounter? The clues are the same, just be careful how you read them. If you are not to be the candidate of choice, urge the interviewer to consider sharing leads with you about where your skills and education might serve a different company more effectively. These referrals are pure gold because this decision maker has interviewed you and knows the market in which you are trying to open opportunities for yourself. If you have favorably impressed this interviewer, leads will be forthcoming.

If you are given leads, be sure to ask the decision maker if you might use his or her name as a source for entering another company's offices to talk with a decision maker there. If at all possible, try to get the interviewer to give you a name of a manager or department head who would understand your background, education, and experience and would know where to put your collected talent to good use in the new company.

The interviewer may be willing to work with you and help you build your network because he or she has been favorably impressed by you, your interaction with them, your skills, education, and experience.

The interviewer may be willing to work with you and help you build your network because he or she has been favorably impressed by you, your interaction, your skills, education, and experience. This person has no immediate need for your talent and is willing to share with another manager in the field or industry. Good decision makers try not to give away the store of talent that might be needed elsewhere in the industry.

Be sure you distinguish that you are not asking them to refer you to the other party, because they do not know you well enough to do that. What you want is for them to refer an industry leader or manager to you, so you can present your own case to that new person. Networks are only as strong as their numbers and the substance of the referrals.

At this point, I offer a word about rejection. If you do not ask for a job, you cannot be rejected. Nevertheless, most candidates have their hopes up going into an interview. If you know there is a job opening there, make your best case for your skill-matching capabilities to the job description. If they do not offer you the position, petition them to help you expand your network. The name of the game is still "not what you know, but who you know." The point is to expand the pool of people you know in the industry of choice.

People are successful in job searches because they are in the right place at the right time, with the right credentials. If there is no job there, one cannot be offered to you. If you do not have sufficient credentials for a position, it will not be offered to you. Your best shot is to get inside the door with a decision maker and make your best case. Those who succeed have often been in the right place, but at the wrong time at one time or another. Some have often been in the wrong place at the right time. The point is that to succeed you must keep on searching. The alternative is not pretty.

Suppose you are meeting someone much younger than you are, possibly a Gen-Xer. Know this ahead of time. You can tell from pictures or by asking the receptionist when this person celebrated their tenth anniversary with the company. Whatever you do, avoid the grunge stereotype that younger generations seem to portray in the movies and on television. You will not be hired in corporate America acting like that, nor do Gen-X managers hire grunge types.

Be creative and talk about your Web skills. Be honest and showcase these skills if you have them. Do not try a hard sell with these younger people. They can smell a phony miles away. If they have reached the management level, you can assume they must be pretty good at "reading people." Be provocative and you will impress them with your ideas and your creativity. They will not be impressed or frightened of your age and prior accomplishments. What they will do is evaluate your credentials, skills, and experience against their immediate needs.

First Impressions

Psychologists of various stripes tell us that it takes less than a minute for a new person to size you up. The impression may be flawed but it will last. Your appearance, your demeanor, and the first words that come out of your mouth are the substance of that first impression, so you really are in charge of the first impression. Nonetheless, an attractive outward appearance cannot hide poor language skills or bad communication habits. All need to be in top order.

When measuring whether you are the ideal candidate, consider: Do you have what they are looking for? Has the position you are discussing been budgeted by the department? Does the person with whom you are interviewing have the authority to make the decisions and the power to negotiate with you? If it is a group decision, try to find out how much influence this interviewer has in the group. Do you get the feeling that this individual trusts you and what you have presented as your qualifications for the position?

A few tips for the first encounter include the following:

- Be direct and interesting in your introduction.
- Do not brag about your accomplishments. Introduce them as dialogue.
- Devise an interesting way to talk about your skills and education.
- Having done good research, find something of special interest to this interviewer's company.
- Develop your opening paragraph and memorize it. Add energy and interest in your voice when you talk about it.
- Make what you say enticing, but don't make your presentation unbelievable.
- Tie what you say to your résumé no matter what format the interviewer has seen.

The Real World

You do live in the real world! No company is going to be a perfect fit for you and your accumulated skills, education, and experience. Frequent complications come crashing in on business operations today from all corners. Business is international, national, and local. Companies may be on one level of operations in a given week or month, and soon they move to another level, often without properly preparing their employees for the move. The forces are mergers, multitiered workforces, cultural diversity, and mobility. To meet these needs, a manager must deal with individuation of employees, groups and teams, and an advanced education force. Top this with corporate behavior that is part of the global image, and you will see that business today is very complicated.

You have a series of tools to compete in this environment. The goal is not to become so distracted that you lose sight of your own professional aims. You have a degree—possibly certification. You are continuing to develop skills you will take with you to the next position you hold. You have experienced a great variety of working tools and methods in your preparation as well as your professional life on your first job.

There are problems in some companies with ethics. The question you might ask yourself when confronted with controversy in your company is, "Just because I can, should I?" This is a simple question but it will help you orient yourself into considering whether the company is asking you to do something unethical according to your standards. Seek advice from wise people outside and inside the company. Then you can decide whether to stay with the corporation or understand it is time to move elsewhere.

Seek advice from wise people outside and inside the company.

Your market potential lies in your plan. The plan is your studied and researched approach to the marketplace of your choice. Your decisions will be acceptable and assist you in your career if you continue to monitor your approach to your career development and to the career path that is best for you.

Continuing Research

Light reading, anyone?

Books

Bridges, William. *Job Shift: How to Prosper in a Workplace Without Jobs.* New York: Perseus Press. 1995.

Davis, Stanley M., Christopher Meyer, and Stan Davis. *Blur: The Speed of Change in a Connected Economy.* New York: Little Brown & Company (Warner Book Edition). 1999.

Samuelson, Pamela and Peter G. Neumann. *Intellectual Property in the Age of Universal Access.* Association for Computing Machinery. 1999.

Senge, Peter M. *The Fifth Discipline: The Art and Practice of the Learning Organization.* New York: Doubleday. 1994.

Wheatley, Margaret J. and Byron Kellner-Rogers. *A Simpler Way.* New York: Berrett-Koehler Publishing. 1998.

Try these sites

General Web Sites and Access Terms

www.about.com
(Access: "college grad markets," "24/7 marketing," "electronic marketing")

www.altavista.com
(Access: "market," "contemporary market potential," "global marketing")

www.askjeeves.com
(Access: "What are global markets?" "What does 24/7 mean?" "What is good voice mail?")

www.dogpile.com
(Access: "International business," "U.S. marketing potential")

www.google.com
(Search with keywords for best results)

General Business and Marketing Sites

www.fastcompany.com

www.4work.com

www.coachu.com

www.careers.wsj.com

www.fiveoclockclub.com

www.oppworld.com

www.jobdocnews.com

CHAPTER 9

Entrepreneurship

Entrepreneurship comes from the French word *entreprendre* (to undertake). It has made its way into the American business vocabulary. It refers to those women and men who take on the risks of realizing their capital venture dreams. This means that they are willing to build a new business enterprise, assuming leadership of its development and understanding the personal and monetary risks involved. Most entrepreneurs are adventuresome, imaginative, and creative individuals. They are willing to gamble on an idea that has not yet been realized in the marketplace.

Entrepreneurs are speculative thinkers who will gamble with an idea, or a chance to create a business where the stakes may be hazardous. Given these odds, it is imperative that the entrepreneur is prepared, has an established business plan that will work, employs the best possible talent the budget will allow, and is committed to sticking with the enterprise to its completion. This activity is usually attempted by 2 percent of American dreamers, only a portion of whom will succeed. Examples today include Mary Kay Ash, Michael Dell, Bill Gates, Ross Perot, Martha Stewart, and Oprah Winfrey.

Try the inventory in Appendix A. You may want to use the data and reflections to determine if you have entrepreneurial tendencies. Becoming an entrepreneur is not the same as becoming a business owner. One can be a business owner through inheritance or buying an existing business. Business ownership, whether as an entrepreneur or otherwise, does equip the individual for this type of enterprise.

Steps to Own Your Own Business

The following list covers the basics:

- Learn as much as you can about the business/industry before you leap.
- Build a 3-year business plan indicating profit margins and personnel needs.
- Remember: No matter how well you budget, this enterprise will always cost more.
- Study and understand the competition. They are ahead of you at the beginning.
- Location is paramount.
- Image is perception.

Owning or starting your own business requires capital investment. Always try to find others to help finance your ideas or your business purchase. The resources are many and varied: banks, venture capitalists, investment groups, and others. Consult with these resources before beginning the venture. If your 3-year plan looks good and worth the investment, you will have some takers. I know Steve Jobs and Steve Wozniak began with $500 in their garage, but their success is not typical.

Buying a business that is a "bargain" often is the equivalent of buying a bad business that will only get worse. What happens to a business when it changes ownership can be compared to an individual who has a heart attack. Many people may survive, but they will have severe limitations to their previous lifestyle and energy level. If the business is already a "bargain," then it will only get worse after you purchase it. So buy a business that is doing well. Any firm you purchase will also have that "heart attack," but a well-run business will be able to sustain the attack because it will be in good business health before you bought it. Check out some good seminars on how to buy a business before you spend all that energy and someone else's cash. You may discover you would rather work for someone else and take your pension when you retire.

Buying a business that is a "bargain" often is the equivalent of buying a bad business that will only get worse.

Consulting

Now let's return to the loner types. How would you know if you want to be a consultant in the field of your major or interest? You must be a great self-motivator because there is no one else in the business but you. You are the marketer, the sales force, the deliverer of services or products, the ombudsman who fixes the complaints; you are everything and everyone. At least hire a secretary!

Organize your business by keeping accurate records. This will come in handy when you need to pay your taxes. It is even more valuable if the IRS decides to audit you, your home business, or your one-person consultancy. These are all frequent targets for IRS audits. You must demonstrate proof for every deduction and business expense you took. No record equals no deduction, plus a penalty.

The smaller your office is (half of your basement or garage), the more it needs to be organized. It is very difficult to be in a one-person business. Everything is your responsibility; every customer problem is yours to solve. There are no limits to the demands on your time and energies because there is nowhere else to go but to you for help with your services or products.

The following will help you to be a great consultant:

- Decide whether you can assume all of this responsibility by yourself.
- Design great brochures and business cards.
- Work hard to get your first client.
- Listen to the need; tackle the situation; close when you have finished.
- Keep in touch with your clients (newsletters, notices, changes)
- Handle all difficulties professionally and promptly.
- If you can't remedy the situation, recommend someone who can.
- Relay your experience and education for customer insight and trust factors.

Always remember that people hire consultants to do something they cannot do, or do not have the time to do, or never want to do again themselves. In all three of these scenarios, it is possible that they know what needs to be done. So do not talk down to your customers about what the problem is. If they have questions about your solutions, talk it over rationally with them. If they become displeased with something you are doing in the process, you will have made a bad impression if you just throw up your hands and say, "Fix it yourself."

Always remember that people hire consultants to do something they cannot do, or do not have the time to do, or never want to do again themselves.

Your customers are smart; they may even know your field very well, so do not underestimate their knowledge when they ask you to explain something about your process, your reasoning, or your conclusions about how to handle a situation. Customers do not expect to be insulted by a professional they have hired to help them with some issue or problem. If you have a creative bent and often do things contrary to conventional wisdom, warn your clients of your approach and explain why it works from your perspective. They may decide to decline your help or to applaud you. In either case you have saved yourself and them headaches and misunderstandings about your professionalism. You may lose the customer, but not your reputation, which is more important.

Business Practice

- Organize and manage money, paper trails, time, staff, legalities, and insurance well.
- Set your fees to be competitive:

- Hourly rates or flat rates for job completion.
- Personal expenses incurred because of the job.
- Raise your rates with the economic trends in your community.
- Consider variable rates for seniors and students to accommodate variety.
- Present the bill upon job completion; collect money at the time agreed.

- Market yourself with eye-catching materials and practices. Be different!
- Qualify your clients before you accept the job; use clear/comprehensive contracts.
- Sell what you know and nothing more.
- Use computer technology and software to keep track of your business.
- Maintain and use a mailing list of your customers to keep them aware of you.
- Keep accurate accounting records of revenues and invoices.
- Prepare fresh presentations using new materials.
- Market electronically over the Internet on the World Wide Web.
- Create a fantastic Web site, especially if you offer Webmaster services.

Whatever you do, practice your profession ethically. "Would you want someone to service your needs the way you assist others?" is always a good measure of ethics. Manage your stress well to project a professional demeanor.

Remember that you can also seek consultants for the help you need. SCORE (Service Corp of Retired Executives) is a group of professional retired entrepreneurs who have been trained to assist individuals who want business management help. The services are free for the asking, and there are offices all across the country. They can be reached on the Web: **www.score.org.** You may also need some consultants from time to time:

- a lawyer to make sure you have not dug yourself into a huge legal hole.
- an accountant to keep your taxes paid on time.
- a graphic artist to create your business cards and brochures.
- a Webmaster to create a Web site for you.

Here's the Deal

Businesses are complex. Running your own business often causes headaches. If you are starting your business from scratch, then count on 5 years to succeed. If you have bought a successful business, count on 2 years after the "heart attack" to consider yourself successful. If you want to start your consultant work as a part-time job (moonlight), then you are ready to leave your full-time job if and when your part-time work equals more than one-half your full-time pay.

The ordinary way a successful business story runs is as follows:

- First year, you are in the red.
- Second year, you can meet most of your bills on time and your payroll.
- Third year, you are able to pay all expenses on time, including bank loans and payroll.
- Fourth year, you may pay all invoices and expenses on time; you may show a little profit.

■ Fifth year, your business is doing well, profits continue and are available for reinvestment.

In all of this discussion about employment as a consultant, what you have to worry about is not whether you can get employment, but rather: Are you employable? This means continuing education and certification in your field/industry. Careers no longer move in smooth and predictable progressions. Today's employees must be flexible, elastic, adaptive, and prepared for adverse circumstances over the course of their employment.

Today's employees must be flexible, elastic, adaptive, and prepared for adverse circumstances over the course of their employment.

Entrepreneurs are willing to go where no one else has dared. But if you do not have an inspired idea or creative concept, all you will see is the risk and that may defeat you. Entrepreneurs are mentally tough and need to be. It is not an exercise for business lightweights. Entrepreneurs with the "right stuff" don't think negatively about taking risks or about getting rich. They are obsessed with building something better or something new, and this obsession drives them to overcome the negative factors that drown lesser pursuers of ideas.

Keep your skills sets current.

- Ask others for their ideas.
- Seek honest feedback, even when it is negative.
- Monitor trends in your industry.
- Build hard and soft skills all along the way. You can never have too many.
- Seize opportunities for informal learning: projects, seminars, role models.
- Conduct informational interviews, at least one weekly.
- Set specific goals for yourself and your company.
- Think globally. The international world is looking for talent also.
- Be proactive. Most people see things and react, not you. Be ahead of the game.
- Habitually read the newest information about your field/industry.

Quitting

Today the literature is replete with examples of people who have ditched a job and found great success elsewhere. Over and over we hear, "Don't quit. It's too risky. How will you pay your bills and honor your accumulated responsibilities?" The case for quitting lies in the current economic boom we see all around us. Individuals are in the stock market making money without brokers. It's not for everyone, but it is happening.

There is an undeniable pleasure in ceasing to do something onerous, even if it pays well. A good maxim to remember is "Finishing what you started is a useful and meritorious course of action only if what you have started is worth finishing." The answer to "Is it worth all this?" only becomes apparent after you have started on a journey to achieve something. People who have reached the pinnacle of their careers are beginning to toss it all and settle for a quiet spot in the woods next to a stream. Why do this? The *Wall Street Journal* claims that 14 percent voluntarily leave their jobs today, the highest rate since the 1980s.

Philosophically look at this phenomenon, and you can see something beyond "quitting" alone. The unprecedented state of the economy encourages individuals who have entrepreneurial dreams to start new things. Examples include a wide variety of people from Silicon Valley, Webmasters who create animated and highly diverse Web pages for individuals and businesses, and those individuals who have insight into the stock market and its wanderings. All of this newness is very exciting, and people are more willing to step out of their small, confining 6' × 8' cubicles and try their wings in a new field while they have the opportunity.

Statistically we know that the most prosperous region (Silicon Valley) in the most prosperous nation (the United States) is also the world's capital for quitting. Even in this location, "quitter" has a negative connotation. This does not mean that the commitment of the workers in Silicon Valley is jaded. They will work very hard and be very committed to the tasks at hand but in a few short years will be off to conquer other fields and interests. "We have not here a lasting city."

Evan Harris presents a sound case in his book, *The Quit: A Consideration of the Art of Quitting* (Simon & Schuster). His advice can be summed up in "Get out while you can!" However, he stretches that injunction with "Consider getting out the minute it crosses your mind." Why waste your time complaining, moaning, and whining about how awful things are? Why must your colleagues tolerate your grouchy, omnipresent commentary about how inadequately one is compensated for time and energy expended? You annoy your colleagues with your bad attitude and your grumbling responses to everything that crosses your desk by memo or e-mail. You constantly have an unpleasant refrain. Reasons to quit are innumerable but the high raters include: stasis, exhaustion, crisis intervention, prove a point, test your own mettle, driven to it, inspired by something else, and because you can. So the question remains, "Do you have the nerve to quit and the motivation or inspiration to do something else more satisfying?" Time will tell.

Entrepreneurs and the people with special gifts for stress management and creative ideas lead very exciting lives, or so it appears to those outside the entrepreneur's environment. It takes a lot of work to master entrepreneurship, and it is an ongoing process that does lead to success and often to great satisfaction. Just remember that it is not for everyone. Bring balance to your decisions and don't stay too long in a venture that is going nowhere. At the same time, evaluate whether what you have started is now worth finishing. Then you are ready to balance your career choices.

Continuing Research

Light reading, anyone?

Books

Culley, Tom. *Beating the Odds in Small Business.* New York: Fireside/Simon & Schuster. 1998.

Herman, Roger. *Keeping Good People.* Greensboro: Oakhill Press. 1989.

Jaffe, Azreila. *Honey, I Want to Start My Own Business: A Planning Guide for Couples.* New York: HarperBusiness. 1997.

Lewis, Michael. *The New New Thing: A Silicon Valley Story.* New York: W. W. Norton. 1999.

Lonier, Terri. *Working Solo.* New York: Wiley. 1998.

Outlaw, Wayne. *Smart Staffing: How to Hire, Reward, and Keep Top Employees in Your Growing Company.* Upstart Publishing Company. 1998.

Thompson, John and Catherine A. Henningsen. *The Portable Executive: Building Your Own Job Security from Corporate Dependency to Self-Direction.* New York: Simon & Schuster. 1996.

Journals

McMorrow, John. "Ten Tips for Keeping Your Skill Set Current." *Solutions*, June 1999. Pages 52–53.

Nakache, Patricia. "Joe Blow Stakes His Claim.com." *Fortune*, June 7, 1999. Pages 217–218.

O'Reilly, Brian. "What It Takes to Start a Start-up." *Fortune*, June 7, 1999. Pages 135–140.

Try these sites

Electronic Commerce Research

www.4work.com

www.score.org

www.fastcompany.com

www.cisco.com

www.sba.gov

www.nbia.org

CHAPTER 10

Business Politics

Office and business politics cause more heat than light in any organization. Politics is the raw pursuit of power. Most people see politics as something others do to them. Unfortunately, or fortunately as the case may be, we are all involved in the politics of the situations we are in if there are two or more people in the workgroup. If you are schizoid, you may create a one-person political disaster by yourself, but then that would be a situation for another discipline to analyze.

Why do people seek power? There are multiple reasons. Power is needed to make decisions, move a company along on a more adventuresome and innovative path, or to slow the pace a bit. People who have an idea or vision of where a company may go in the future want to see their visions realized. In order to make their vision real, they want the power to control the outcome of their perception. These individuals build a power base of supporters and do their best to keep their cohorts happily following the leader.

Job reviews, job changes, promotions, new projects, and succession charts are among a few of the tools that companies use to "control" their workforces with rewards. The more clear the path to a specific reward, the more takers there will be for it. If the race for vice president of marketing is aligned with the education and experience factors required for the position, those interested can prepare to become that vice president if the current position is vacated for some reason. If employees are sure that the selection process is fair, they will usually accept the new appointment without much rumor mongering. When employees are not sure of what it takes to become a vice president, and it isn't broadcast where everyone can see it, then the HR director is inviting speculation and rumors will follow. This also makes it bad for the new appointee to face the resistance of others for something in which he or she was not involved.

When looking for a good company, you want to know how its politics work.

When looking for a good company, you want to know how its politics work. The culture of the company is a good source to study. Large corporations may have several intertwined cultures.

An example would be a company that requires advanced degrees or certification of some of its employees, but a high school diploma is sufficient for others; those going to school while continuing to work make up another cultural group. Some companies are hi-tech for product and service to customers, whereas the home office is a more traditional office-type culture. The differences usually show when some executive decides that the company employees should be more chummy and friendly, so gatherings and events are planned in which all are to participate. These are doomed to be disasters, considered a waste of time by some while satisfying others, thus furthering the divide between working groups in the company.

This is important for you to understand because the politics of the working business day and who socializes with whom, when and where leads to decisions made "outside the box." Employees not in the loop only look with amazement and begin to gossip about the how and the why of the appointment, but they do not know the who, where, when, and why of the decision. No wonder companies are hurt by gossip. This is well deserved if HR practices are hidden from the general workforce, and things "just happen" from the employees' point of view.

Because you have a degree, most employers will hire you as a knowledge worker. This fact alone separates you from all those employees who do not have a degree, or are working toward one, but don't have it yet. There are technical workers who find themselves unable to communicate with "those other employees." When a company has these uneven levels of professional development within its walls, the time is ripe for gossip and rumor. Without communication, politics can get a bad name. Diplomacy and tact are needed everywhere. Those with these specific "soft skills" will be considered political and will usually be good at it.

Promotion

Making it to the top is a political action, no matter the environment. If you cannot picture yourself at the top of your game, you probably will not reach it. This is because the real dividing line is passion. Good politicians have passion to sustain everything else they must do to win. Pick your team members and companions carefully whenever you have the chance. These people will be your support for as high as you want to go. Failing has more to do with not nailing that last 5 percent than it does with the whole battle. Of course, without the strategy of the fight, there is nothing to nail down during the last 5 percent.

If you cannot picture yourself at the top of your game, you probably will not reach it.

Those in executive and managerial positions are always making judgments about the workforce. The decision makers must be confident in their ability to decide. That will happen if the decision maker relies on evidence and facts, and not on gut instincts. If you are a decision maker, work hard at not making other people's decisions; you will have plenty of your own. Making more decisions than you need to is why a managerial day is so long and the other employees can go home on time. Managers mistakenly take the burden and move to accept responsibility for a worker's job because the employee has politically empowered the manager to do the worker's job. Excuses sound like, "I just don't have time." "I'm already overburdened with other work." "I just don't know how to do this." Rather than manage the situation so the employee does the work, the employer or manager does the work.

How will you know if you or your manager is a good decision maker? Good decisions are the product of two ideas. The view of one's world is the first. "How is this situation to turn out?" is the first question in the decision maker's mind. What strategy will enable the vision to become a reality is the second. But these two are not cause and effect; indeed they must be married in the decision maker. If this happens the individual will almost always make good decisions.

Now let's transfer this concept to one's personal life. You are in a career search that is part of your whole career development and balanced with your life goals. This is not a mathematical equation. For this level of decision making, one needs a deeper level of consciousness or awareness. You have developed an inner wisdom from prior decisions you have made about your life. There are patterns here. Explore these patterns and see what the common feelings are. Then join these together with whatever hard data you may have to make your personal decisions. It takes courage to listen to your inner wisdom, but that is where you live. So take the plunge and trust yourself on this. It will take time, effort, and patience to accompany that courage but you can do it.

Political Interaction

Questions to ask interviewers about the intellectual development of staff fall in three general categories. Does the company retain repositories for its best practices and new learning gained from the day-to-day operations as well as the project satisfaction of clients? Is there a method whereby individual workers in a company can access that database or interact with other successful employees to create new products or processes? Are their formal steps where lessons learned while implementing a new process or creating a project for a client can then be shared with others? If yes, how is this done? And if no, why not?

Politics is most active in these three areas. There are some things that may be proprietary. Most things can be shared about process. Client projects will rely on the combined knowledge of the firm to assist the responsible team to arrive at the best decision for the customer. Keeping things to oneself defeats the purpose of collegiality. It also fosters linear and minutely focused thinking. There are companies today that benchmark, or even share their process and product information with their competitors to make better products and services for the customers.

The best tools for benchmarking and sharing information within an organization and outside the organization are the Intranet and Internet capabilities of modern technology. Those individuals who are good at sharing information become popular and are considered knowledgeable within the walls of the company and frequently among customers, who will ask for a specific team to work on their project.

Now we come to Internet-based or videoconferencing meetings in which people are not in the same location, but they are attending a meeting. If you know the meeting is going to be a conference call, you must prepare doubly for the meeting. The agenda should be known in advance. This enables all the participants to come to their desktops and video screens prepared to participate.

If you are able, prepare some visual options that you can incorporate on the other participants' screens to keep the group focused on your ideas. Minds can wander when all are in the same room together; think of the options for wandering when the conference participant is alone. The meeting facilitator is most responsible, but each individual can do something specific to make the audio work to advantage. Obviously the ones with greatest political advantage here are those who feel comfortable with cyberspace communication.

It is becoming a truism that the faster we go, the less we honor the human interchange and the more disconnected we become from each other. Rudeness is rising. Society is becoming dissonant. Humans no longer act or decide humanely. Managers continue multitasking while an employee is trying to get an answer. Politicians are advised by their hired consultants to campaign negatively by using falsehoods and fear tactics. These are all variations on a theme about our times. You know when your behavior is getting out of line with your own values and ethics. You also can judge when to object to someone else's crude behavior.

Your behavior is in your control. Watch your language. Four-letter words abound, along with other vulgarities, but you don't have to use them. The lexicon is rich enough to express your ideas and feelings adequately. Avoid sarcasm and do not use words such as "Whatever" as a response or reaction to a situation or a question. Try not to escalate a conflict if one is brewing.

It is a classic response but try to rephrase, repeat, and reflect what the rude commentary has been with a question in your voice. The boss, while sailing into your cubicle, has just accused you of blowing a report, falsifying the numbers, or missing them altogether. Your response is to stay cool and ask, "I blew the report?"

Confront the individual, involve yourself in the solution, and problem solve together.

"I falsified numbers?" "I missed some of the numbers?" What you are communicating is that you got the message but you need more information in order to clarify exactly what the manager is implying. Do you need to explain or resign?

On the other hand you are no one's doormat, nor should you be. So pick when and where you will respond with anger, without being angry (a good trick if you can do it). Use the adrenaline that is inspiring you to deck your opponent and take a time-out—rest room, soft drink, run around outside the building, cool down, chill out—then respond directly with whatever the issue at stake is. Confront the individual, involve yourself in the solution, and problem solve together. This takes discipline and goodwill on both individuals' parts.

You are never responsible for changing other people's behavior, even if you are the boss. A cubicle mate listens to talk radio all day, and the volume is too high for the open 6' by 8' cubicles we must work in these days. Instead of telling her the radio is a nuisance, tell her why the volume level of her radio is interfering with your concentration or telephone calls. Then consult together about what can be done to accommodate both of you. If one side or the other unilaterally decides that there will be no negotiating, that one side is right, you may need an arbitration hearing. Some individuals are just recalcitrant and are sure they are the only ones with any good ideas or have some primacy because of who they think they are in the organization.

You are never responsible for changing other people's behavior, even if you are the boss.

In today's work world, there are coaches hired from outside the company to deliver bad news about a colleagues' offensive body odor, constant talkativeness, or excessive or overwhelmingly odiferous perfume or after shave lotion use. These coaches can be hired for a nominal fee, usually about $15 to $20 and will deliver the message anonymously over the Internet or snail mail. The message will be diplomatically worded.

Employees do not want to offend their coworkers, they don't want to create problems, but they wish someone would tell the offensive persons about their disagreeable behaviors. Sensible civility tracks the tension between freedom and morality. Sometimes you may just have to tolerate the conduct of someone whose behavior you find worthy of opprobrium. This tension is a mark of a nation that declares itself free.

Getting Vested

Moving up in a company is a political action. How do you get a piece of the action you are creating? Knowledge workers can see and feel the direct relationship between the work they do and the market value of the company. Attitudes toward jobs are changing, and knowledge workers are at the leading edge of that change.

The biggest and first option to negotiate is a satisfactory stock option. This can be done before you join a firm. Remember: "You don't get what you deserve, but what you negotiate!" Companies capitalize on the naiveté of graduates and new people to their company culture. The value point for negotiating 5 percent of annual revenues when joining a start-up company is a matter of equity, and that is important to knowledge workers. If your ideas are going to put the company on the map, you promise to stay and help them succeed for a percentage of the action. They promise to pay you the percentage when the company figures its profits at the end of the year.

Remember: "You don't get what you deserve, but what you negotiate!"

How does this all work, you may wonder? There are some things to remember. Usually only 40 percent of start-up companies ever go public, and most that do go public do not amount to much. For every Microsoft there are 20 dogs just lapping along, barking all the way.

The number of zeros in your stock option grant means nothing. What really matters is the percentage of the company that you own. To illustrate this point: A graduate engineer, when a company offered him stock options on

50,000 shares, adamantly insisted on 100,000 shares because a colleague had gotten 100,000 shares from his new company. Not knowing the value of the shares of these two companies in question, the novice engineer was looking at the number of zeros. He could not be dissuaded. The hiring company did a four-for-one stock split and gave him the 100,000 he insisted upon, and they were amazed that he was so happy with half the value they had originally offered him. It's not the zeros!

Timing is important. The best time to negotiate a percentage of ownership is within 6 to 18 months before the company goes public. A year after an initial public offering (IPO), stock value is 5 percent to 10 percent of what it will be at the public offering. There is an automatic ramp-up in the share price at that time.

You are not the only person in the company, so don't make demands as if you were. Equity is fairness. If a company has hired two knowledge workers ahead of you for 1 percent of equity, they will not hire you for 1.5 percent of equity. It would not be fair and it would destroy morale in the company. You are negotiating into a familial group at start-up time. Whatever you negotiate becomes public information at the moment of the IPO.

Negotiating for equity is the most direct way to get a piece of the action. But options simply are not the same for everyone. Sun Microsystems, once a high-flying start-up, is currently struggling to keep their top talent as more and more stock-happy start-up companies are making fantastic offers. Sun will turn shares into cash based on profits the project generates at the end of a fixed time period (3–5 years) in order to keep their talent. It puts a premium on timely performance. With this program an engineer or computer scientist can make a lot of money, but only if they are committed to sticking with the company. If the knowledge worker leaves, they lose their investment. Sun Microsystems wants its people to feel that they can stay with Sun and win.

www.askjeeves.com has the best explanation of phantom stocks. This is a paraphrase of their ideas: Phantom stock seems like the logical solution. Instead of actually giving people stock in the company, you promise to pay them a cash bonus at some future point equal to a certain percentage of the company's equity. The bonus has the same tax consequences to them and the company as any other bonus. There are no rules limiting how much you can give on what basis or to whom. There are no requirements to have your stock valued, so you can just use a formula your CPA cousin devises. Employees will have their financial well-being tied to the growth of the company, but with a minimum of bother.

Continuing: The downside is figuring out how much phantom stock to give out. If the first 10 people each get phantom stock worth 1 percent of the equity, do the next 10 get the same? Does this mean new people soon will not be able to be included because the company eventually will owe its entire equity value in cash? The equity of the company must be valued, and there is the issue of funding the obligation. Does the company just make a promise to pay, or does it really put aside the funds? The most difficult issues, however, are regulatory.

Do you need an agent? It really depends on your track record coming out of school, senior projects, work while you went to school, degree earned, certifications held, and volunteer work. It is absolutely routine today for software developers, computer games creative pioneers, and interactive CD-ROM designers to use cyberagents to negotiate on their behalf. The agent usually does this for 10 percent of the value of the total compensation negotiated. If you know the answers to the following four questions and you feel confident in your answers, then you are probably ready to negotiate for yourself. After you have a bit more experience, you may want to revisit the cyberagent issue again.

- How valuable are you, really? (Know if you are a "tent pole" in the company or not.)
- How can you put yourself in play? (Your strategy should stimulate competition. You must put yourself in an auction. Who needs you?)
- What risks will you take? ("If I increase sales from $1 million to $10 million in two years, double my salary.")
- How thorough are you prepared to be? (Think strategically, like a lawyer, a business consultant, and a knowledge worker.)

Upward mobility outranks job security, according to a survey of young workers commissioned by the AFL-CIO to help understand the workforce in the new economy. Only 8 percent were union members at the time of the survey conducted by Peter D. Hart Research Associates. Seventy-two percent of the workers interviewed believe they will work for 2 to 10 employers over their lifetime. The one overarching factor in the job markets today, above all others, is that young Americans must graduate from college to be in full-time jobs with any permanency. Only 50 percent of those young workers without degrees have standard employment. The rest are working part-time, temporary, or substandard arrangements.

Mentor-Protégé Relationships

Mentor-protégé programs have been around for a long time, and many companies take advantage of the opportunities for shepherding along new hires and at the same time introducing new information and tactics to older employees. Differentiating among mentor, coach, and supervisor points out the varied nature of assistance new people might need.

Mentors are sounding boards. They give advice, but it doesn't have to be followed. Mentors are personally involved over the protégés' long-term development. A coach helps someone develop specific skills that are needed. Coaches challenge individuals about performance expectations.

Supervisors were unanimously seen as performance management types, who want to get the job done, by the protégés who cooperated in this survey. Unfortunately in the eyes of many protégés the supervisor collects the negative evaluations within their relationship to the new employee.

In this same national survey measuring effective mentoring, protégés identified the following as things mentors helped them to acquire as well as described their mutual interaction. There is a strong theme of assistance, development, and growth as the protégés' responses were tallied. They see mentors as building personal confidence, empowering the new employees to improve, stimulate their learning with a soft, no-pressure self-discovery methodology. They found that they could share their experiences with the mentors, and through analysis of these experiences, mentors could help them understand their behaviors and learn new ways to behave.

The protégés felt that their mentors had taught them to recognize their own strengths and weaknesses. Mentors were given credit for explaining things well by the protégés. Protégés seemed to appreciate that the mentors did not give them answers, but assisted and supported them to develop and find their own responses. Mentors can be a source of knowledge, but on the order of Socrates. Mentoring highlights adult learning as opposed to the teacher-to-student model with which new employees were all too familiar.

These mentor-protégé relationships are a part of the political relationships that new employees can begin to formulate for themselves. Often mentors are helpful in describing how one can climb the career ladder of a given company successfully. If a success chart has been put together by the HR department, then the mentor can show protégés how they might take advantage of the information on succession planning for their own career development.

> *Protégés seemed to appreciate that the mentors did not give them answers, but assisted and supported them to develop and find their own responses.*

Robert Greene and Joost Eiffers offered a very succinct analysis of the pursuit of power and what they thought of those who engaged in this pursuit ruthlessly. The title of their work is *The 48 Laws of Power* (Viking Press, 1998). Those who lust for power already know these things. But for those of us who do not know these things and find ourselves at the bottom of the heap all the time, we may learn some ways of defending ourselves against them. One suggestion they make is "Power requires the ability to play with appearances. To this end you must wear many masks and keep a bag full of deceptive tricks."

Seek the help of the HR director if you are looking to win at the in-house job-search opportunities. If you have a mentoring program, seek the advice and counsel of your mentor. Let your supervisor know you are interested in improving your career by moving into other areas than the one in which you were initially hired. If someone has been coaching you on improving your skills, elicit their support when you have identified an in-house job you would like to have. In-house job searches are very political by definition.

If the HR director is any good, there will be succession charts (see Figure 10.1), updated about every 6 months, so that all employees can see the

---

FIGURE 10.1   Sample succession chart.

MARKETING	PRODUCTION	FINANCE
Marion Lambert Vice President of Marketing	Allison Fremont Vice President of Production	James MacDonald Vice President of Finance
Jane Lamboth 15 years with company MS in Marketing	Bill Mathews, Foreman 6 years with company Technician Certificate	Mary Anne Finch 2 years in accounting department MA in Accounting, CPA
Susan French (New) Top sales in the industry last year BS in Marketing	Frank Patterson (New) Night Supervisor 1st year with company BS in Management	Ellen Chang 2 years as a bookkeeper BS in Accounting, CPA
Ben Romero Sales Manager BS in Management	Alan Lenier Special Projects Manager 10 years with the company	John Decker (New) One half year in accounting BS in Accounting, CPA

requirements for a given position. If an MBA is needed for the position, but someone with a BA, who seems to be a favorite of the president, gets the job, then everyone knows that hanky-panky is alive and well in the organization. When favorites are hired, they are often dismissed by other employees and lose what authority they may have had. If people see the qualifications and discover that a new hire has all of the qualifications and maybe a few more, the HR office looks good and there is confidence in the fairness of the hiring process.

Money

Many new employees find that they have to pay their dues by serving on call. There are definitions of this term, and they should be negotiated before accepting the position. If an on-call employee can leave the premises and be called back when needed, then compensation is for the time actually serving customers, which is evaluated as paid time for doing whatever is the business of the company. On the other hand, if the nature of being on call requires the employee's presence at the company and the employee may not leave, compensation is due for the hours spent at the company.

Contracts with employees may not contradict the Fair Labor Standards Act (FLSA). This is true even if the employer and the employee agree in a collective bargaining agreement what will be considered hours worked or what payments will be included in the regular rate. If such agreements violate the provisions of the FLSA, they are illegal and subject to civil and criminal penalties. If you think there is a violation where you work, consult a labor lawyer to advise you on a course of action.

If there are violations, an employer can go back for the previous 2 years and correctly compensate employees who were subject to the noncompliance policy. This may seem expensive to the employer, but then look at the costs of government penalties for noncompliance, litigation costs, and back pay likely to result if the employee were to file a complaint with the Department of Labor or bring suit against the company. That would result in serious money and be more costly in the long run.

Want a raise? Be creative. When you read the lists of benefits that companies are offering in compensation packages, it is clear that creativity is at an all-time high. If you think you deserve a raise, you will have to convince the manager. It doesn't always have to be a monetary increase. Look at the benefits side of things. (Reconsider the charts in Chapter 6.)

- Look for ways to get noticed. (Volunteer for projects. Get more training or certification. Develop new skills, then you will be able to show how much you are contributing to the bottom line.)

- Always have documentation. (Research what others with similar skills get paid. Provide benchmarks by which success can be measured—testimonials to achievements.)

- Be careful about your timing. (Save requests for the good times when the company can see now is the time to reward employees. When the budget has been cut, hold your fire unless you can substantiate your contribution.)

The Boss

This is someone you must deal with, whether you like the person or not. No matter what, do not let yourself become a victim of your boss's weaknesses. Keep what you have observed or experienced of your boss's sins to yourself. It does you no good to broadcast them. This makes you a part of a cancer swirl in the workplace.

Keep careful watch over the situations for which you have responsibility and control. Make sure your job is in A+ order. If it isn't, keep improving. Credibility is something you earn gradually by being one of the best performers in your department or business. Develop the habit of being loyal to people in their absence, whether they are your boss or colleagues. Try to understand your boss's perspective and responsibilities. If you are a leader in your own field or department, then you won't have time to bad-mouth others.

A "bad boss" happens to everyone somewhere along the line. Bad bosses have many stripes. They can be bullies, which is management by terror. They may be paranoid and lock themselves up in their offices and are never seen until they leave the building. A good bureaucrat can get things done within the system, but a wimp or an organizational fascist is usually considered crazy by most of the employees. The narcissist sees everything in relation to the way the boss reflects about the egotist's influence and behavior. They are often arrogant and misinformed about their own influence, which frequently becomes its own punishment. You can have a "lover" who considers the position as an opportunity to nurture and encourage all the worst-performing people in the department while preparing to fire them.

> *A "bad boss" happens to everyone somewhere along the line.*

Sometimes plots of employees are needed if any work is to get done when you have a bad boss. Just organize and figure out a way to get plans approved, and then go ahead and keep the department afloat despite the boss. Even if your plots don't work, the camaraderie of your colleagues relieves some of the stress a bit. If it gets too bad, you may just have to bite the bullet and leave. The company leaders usually know you have a bad manager and they will not do anything about it. It is time to leave. Life is too short.

The best advice to follow in political matters is to align yourself with people who share your values in the workplace. If you are having difficulty with someone, learn all you can about that person and try to develop a way to relate, at least on a professional basis. No matter what the issue is, be sure you have set your limits for negotiating. This includes time, space, personnel, and equipment; whatever is shared commonly needs some negotiating and management for all to have adequate access.

Try to show that you are willing to compromise. You are not out for conflict. Whenever you are in charge, people will notice that there is peace, not conflict, when you run the show. If someone tries to bully you, your ideas, or your colleagues in your presence, do not back down from the challenge. Never show fear in these situations. Take a deep breath, but do not lose hold of your values.

It is an important skill to learn to be comfortable with silence. The political ploy of "split the difference" works for no one and puts the decision off to another day; the battle needs to be fought again. Pick the fights you can win. If you find yourself on the edge of a losing argument, let it go. Your real skill will be recognized as a relationship builder, not a conqueror. More people will follow your leadership because they have a relationship with you. Politics is not easy, but it is not astrophysics either. You can be a good political player. Know what you want and what your values are. Make alliances and remember your friends. Good politicians always watch their backs while going forward to reach their own goals.

Continuing Research

Light reading, anyone?

Books

Boston, Thomas D. *Affirmative Action and Black Entrepreneurship.* New York: Routledge. 1999.

Craig, Sue. *Make Your Mark: Influencing Across Your Organization.* New York: McGraw-Hill. 1998.

DeLuca, Joel R. *Political Savvy; Systematic Approaches to Leadership Behind the Scenes.* Evergreen, CO: The Evergreen Business Group. 1999.

Grote, Jim and John McGeeney. *Clever as Serpents: Business Ethics and Office Politics.* Washington, DC: The Liturgical Press. 1997.

Post, Peggy and Peter Post. *The Etiquette Advantage in Business: Personal Skills for Professional Success.* New York: HarperCollins. 1999.

Sabath, Ann Marie. *International Business Etiquette Europe: What You Need to Know to Conduct Business Abroad with Charm and Savvy.* Franklin Lakes, NJ: The Career Press. 1999.

(Ms Sabath has many books, about one a year, on business etiquette at home and around the globe. The above-listed book is her latest.)

Salmon, Rosemary and William A. Salmon. *Office Politics for the Utterly Confused (Office Politics Series).* New York: McGraw-Hill. 1998.

Vault.com (Editor). *Vault Reports Guide to Schmoozing.* New York: Houghton Mifflin. 1998

Journals

Graham, Gerald. "Eliminate Office Politics and End Many Problems in Companies." *Wichita Business Journal.* Wichita: American Cities Business Journals. *Industry News Columns:* Week of February 8, 1998. **www.amcity.com/ wichita/stories/1998/02/09/newscolumn4.html**

Try these sites

Office Politics Links

Duncan, Barbara. *Office Politics.* **www.sandz.com/business/politics/051897. html** 1997.

Gorden, Bill. *On the Right Path to Becoming Political at Work?* **www.gwis.com/~wego/q145.htm** The Workplace Doctors #145.

General Links

www.about.com
  (Small-business information access)

www.altavista.com
  (By topic; the less words the better)

www.askjeeves.com
  (Topic formulated as a question is best.)

www.dogpile.com
  (Search engine of other search engines)

www.google.com
  (Search engine based on keywords)

Financial Literacy

To accomplish the goals of this section and not write an additional complete text on the subject of financial literacy, I forewarn the reader that many definitions are included in numerous charts to make the information better understood. You have met most of these terms in your school life and in your work and family life. Many of the points are elementary and known by most scholars. When you negotiate, strategize, plan, and blueprint your career and life plans, these personal design schemes will be realized with as much savvy and sophistication as possible. How to maximize these concepts for your advantage in career development and life goal visions is the focus of this section.

Chapter 11 reveals some of the innumerable possibilities for investment options. These options and the meaning of the terms used are very important for the graduate to understand because you are going to negotiate some of these options at the beginning of your professional career. You will also be able to alter them as your income increases and your opportunities to invest become a reality. I know that right now you just want to pay off your college loans. But if you invest smartly and with confidence, you will have much more to invest and manage later on in your career and life. Financial literacy begins with a basic understanding of money and taxes.

Chapter 12 reveals some of the mysteries of the 401(k), 403(b), and IRA investment plans that are prevalent in today's workplace. The laws change at the federal level and at the state levels with enough frequency to be worthy of watchfulness. How and when to withdraw funds may not be issues at this point, but they will become crucial in your later years. Some points to understand about Social Security are needed, especially for those who are going to be consultants and free agents in the marketplaces of choice.

Chapter 13 is about investing in your education now and in the future. Would you believe that I am encouraging you to go back to school or to become even more certified than your degree warrants? Yes, continuing education and being picky about where and when you continue gaining educational certifications of your continuing learning are extremely important to advancement in your career.

Lastly, Chapter 14 is about retirement. Some may say, "It can't come soon enough for me." Others may opine, "Why do I need to worry about that now? I'm very young." These are the opposing poles on this continuum. Everyone falls at a different place on that continuum given their work environments, erudition, certification, and the continuing development of their chosen fields.

The closer you are to retirement, the more you will wish you had thought about it earlier and made smarter decisions. Retirement is something those farther away from it do not want to contemplate and, consequently, do not plan for its eventuality.

All of these separate topics make up financial literacy. This section is meant to touch on these topics enough to encourage you to think about them seriously, plan for their eventualities carefully, and finally, enjoy your retirement happily—with good luck and guardian angels' assistance to survive in good health. It may be a career goal to amass whatever money and investments you wish, but it will be the life choices you make that will enable you to live long enough to enjoy the fruits of your planning.

CHAPTER 11

Money and Taxes

Here's the deal: Your money must grow. Where should you put your earned income to work for you? You must learn how and practice ways to preserve and protect your hard-earned money. With this in mind, let's look at things to consider while building assets that will be used in the future to purchase more of what you want or need to have.

Financial Ladder

The financial ladder in Figure 11.1 illustrates the methodology and timing of your investments so that you have what you need before you become speculative with the potential that is available to you for investments. Stages one and two present the bare bones of investment and the beginning of financial success. Stages three through five align those investments with some manageable risk once the first two stages are successfully in hand. Stages six through eight are about high risk and gambling with your investments. These investment options are not for everyone, but may be useful for you. Move slowly and judiciously. Educate yourself and continuously seek well-balanced and professional advice in these matters.

The financial ladder illustrated on the next page is a long-range look at an investment strategy, continuing familial needs, and future retirement potential. Looking at this chart, one can see that careful moves are to be made if the greatest advantage is to be taken among the options available. The terms are loosely defined. Column one charts the time and place you might consider negotiating for some of these options. As you move along in your career, the financial options are delineated in column two. The third column identifies the levels of risk embedded in the various options. The fourth column illustrates a way familial and personal needs can be thought of as you plan and implement your monetary strategies.

Make Your Money Grow

The following guidelines will help your investment dollars increase:

- It's never too late or too early to begin saving and investing regularly.
- How much should you save? It depends on how old you are.
  - Up to age 40, save or invest approximately 5 percent of your pretax pay.
  - From ages 41 to 45, increase your savings/investments by 1 percent per year.
  - Over 45, savings and investments need to be in the 10 to 15 percent of pretax pay.
- Participate in tax-deferred, company-sponsored plans like a 401(k) or a 403(b).
- In addition, invest on your own with an IRA. (Watch the rules—they keep changing.)
- Best investment for most people is stocks because they frequently pay double what bonds pay on an historical average of 11 percent annually.
- Surest way to invest in stock is to do dollar cost averaging.
- Money that you will not need for the next 3 to 5 years, invest in stocks for the long term.
- Mutual funds are a sensible investment. Begin with a Standard and Poor's stock index fund until you get more familiar with the market.
- Establish a trust fund, even if you do not have a large estate. The state will tax whatever they can if you have not made arrangements before your demise.
- Have enough life, major medical, and special insurance coverage for you and your family's needs.

Financial ladder. **FIGURE 11.1**

STAGE	FINANCIAL OPTIONS	RISK	OBJECTIVES
One	Property, casualty, and liability insurance	Without insurance, the cost of replacement is prohibitive.	Auto, property, casualty, liability protection.
	Life, major medical insurance	Without insurance, earning power is severely reduced.	Protects earning power of family's primary wage earner.
	Health and disability insurance	To cover the high cost of hospitalization and medical care.	Group health and disability plans through employers.
	Emergency funds	10% is a good ratio to achieve.	Savings to cover emergencies.
Two	Personal residence	Ownership brings responsibility.	A win-win situation.
	Retirement plans	No plans, not much future.	IRAs, SEPs, 401(k)s, 403(b)s.
	Specific savings or college funds	Without realistic savings plans, you risk family's and your future needs.	The choice depends on your own family goals.
Three	Income mutual funds	Risky—go slowly and seek professional advice.	Offers fairly consistent dividends and diversity potential.
	Bonds	Be careful where you loan money.	Governed by interest activity.
	Blue-chip stocks	Purchase AAA stocks and bonds.	Focused on dividend returns.
	Government securities	Lowest risk charted.	Interest on loans to governments.
Four	Real estate	Care and management needed.	Direct tax advantage.
	Growth and mutual funds income	Be assured that professional management is qualified.	Diversification with professional management.
	Income limited partnerships	Know your partner's complete history.	Shared income on ownership percentage.
Five	Common stocks	Good place for excess funds.	Excellent inflation hedge.
	Growth mutual funds	Risk comes when you move toward aggressive growth.	Great variety with some aggressive income growth.
Six	Growth limited partnerships	Major risk is the quality of the professional management team.	Movie rights, commercial property, storage units, etc.
	Raw land	Select area with care and forethought.	Usually increases in value annually.
	Collectibles/hard assets	Commissions are quite expensive.	Gold, silver, art collections, precious metals to own.
Seven	Options and warrants	High risk, more like gambling.	Stock options for high return.
	Oil and gas	Very volatile; high gains, high losses.	Exploratory pursuits of gas and oil.
Eight	Commodities	90-day predictions; high risk.	Futures market gambling.

Money Management Help

Along your money management trail, you will need different advice and counsel with different experiences and career activities. The following are tried-and-true money advisors because money is their business. You will find others to assist you with specific monetary advice as your career blossoms and your family grows.

- Visit your banker. Only deal with FDIC-insured banks. Negotiate the highest interest rate.
- Put savings account money into a money market account with compounding interest.
- If you can afford 90-day or higher CDs, move your savings to a CD account.
- Hire a financial planner, but shop and interview carefully about your selection.
- Budget your take-home money monthly.

When you are deciding where your funds are to be allocated, you need to keep three things in mind: (1) if the money is for your children's education and will be needed in the next 3 to 5 years, be sure you have put the money in a super-safe investment such as bonds or money market funds; (2) if you are fairly young, have strong career opportunities, and a long time frame for your investment options, put your money in stocks or mutual funds that invest in stocks; and (3) if you are older, nearing retirement, or in retirement, you may want to invest in bonds, which are more secure, although they are slower-growing investments.

Regardless of your age, it is your mental attitude that plays the biggest part in investing options you will consider.

Regardless of your age, it is your mental attitude that plays the biggest part in investing options you will consider. If you are naturally or historically conservative with money, you will remain so. You will probably be smart to invest conservatively. You will be happier. No one wants to lose sleep over falling stocks in which you are heavily invested in your old age. On the other hand, if you are accustomed to taking financial risks, enjoy supporting new ventures, and have faith in the country's economic leadership, you might want to place a good part of your free cash into stocks. Watch the market and trade with care and education. Due to the longer life expectancy of our senior citizens (100,000 U.S. citizens are over 100 years old), you may want to keep some stocks or stock mutual funds in your portfolio at all times.

Keep this Wall Street saying in your mind's eye: "Bears make money, bulls make money, but hogs do not make money." No one is prescient enough to predict the market highs and lows, but watching the market carefully will enable you to make some pretty good guesses.

Finance Scams

A few words about financial scams are important here. Scams can begin as an innocent phone call or Internet message on your computer. Maybe you received one of those infamous chain letters in your e-mail. All of them promise you easy money and frequently lots of it. Very smart and educated people have been duped out of thousands of dollars with these financial scams. The perpetrators are frequently caught, but not soon enough to protect some family or individual from losing their savings in a scam.

Some points to keep in mind.

- If it sounds too good to be true, it probably is.
- If the offer is legitimate, the business will be willing to answer all your questions, however many there may be. So make a list.
- Take your time to decide. Reputable companies will not press you for an immediate answer or threaten withdrawal of the offer after 48 hours.
- If you have the slightest hint of discomfort about what is being sold or the manner in which you are being sold the product or service, don't buy it.
- Report fraud as soon as you are aware that you have been had to the proper authorities.
- Do not fear the risk of embarrassment about admitting that you have been swindled. If everyone did that, then we would all lose and the crooks would never be caught.

Investing for Your Children's Education

Here you are reading about putting away money you haven't even earned yet, into a fund for the college education of children you do not have yet. You are thousands of dollars in debt, and the news is you must save and invest for the future now. Think of the cost of your education. Some prognosticators are predicting that your children will need approximately $250,000 each for their college education. Where are you going to save a quarter of a million dollars for each child's education? They better be smart kids and earn scholarships, or you need to start saving today at compound interest to build a great savings pool for your family needs.

The following guidelines will help you provide a college education for your children who want to go to college.

- Encourage the child to work through high school and save for a college education.
- You will still need to negotiate some loans to assist them with their education costs.
- Loan options are legion and some are tax deductible.
- Dip into retirement savings only as a last resort. You are going to need that money.
- Put the money in your name, not the child's name.
- No matter your income, apply for financial aid at the college of your choice.
- Negotiating pays off big here. Knowledge of what is possible needs to be clarified with the financial aid officer. Understand all the time frames, payback options, and interest changes.
- Compare colleges and see what they have to offer by way of financial assistance. Community college costs may offer considerable savings. Be sure their earned credits are acceptable at 4-year schools.

- Don't overlook private scholarships, merit-based financial aid, government education grants, loans, and military aid for education.

Debt Reduction

Credit cards are a blessing and a curse. They are easier to get than ever. Students line up to gain access to this "easy money" when the hawkers come to sell their credit card wares. Credit card debt, more than any other kind of debt, will keep you from financial security. Individuals and families live from paycheck to paycheck because of credit card buying habits usually started in late high school or college.

Credit cards are a blessing

and a curse.

Other things may happen to cause your debt to soar, but you can control credit card spending. You have college loans to pay back. Medical expenses for you or members of your family, with or without insurance are astronomical. A sudden job loss means no money coming in, and whatever money there is soon disappears. The unforeseen carburetor failure or some more expensive things gone wrong with your car can be a large bill. The list is endless, but the one debt you have most control over is credit card debt.

You need a plan.

- Identify what you buy with credit cards and cut back on those items.
- Where possible, and only as a short-term solution, combine all your credit card debt into one payment plan and pay it down to $0.
- Make the monthly payback amount the highest you can afford, and when possible add a little more to the principal to pay early.
- If you are hooked on a credit card, switch to a debit card. That transaction comes out of your bank account immediately.
- If these tips don't work for you, seek credit card counseling services.

Fantastic Plastic? Not So Fast

Kinds of cards available:

- Low-interest premium cards are only best if you carry a balance.
- No-fee premium cards are best if you usually pay the full balance each month.
- Rebate cards are the best kind of cash-back cards.

    Back-door credit card expenses: low rates that suddenly leap:

- Happens when banks sell their accounts to other banks.
- Can jump when your balance rises above $2,000.
- Banks tack on high fees for exceeding credit limits.
- You pay higher interest rates for cash advances, plus a cash advance fee.
- Late payments can cause high charges plus a hike in interest rates.

Some credit card issuers seem bent on alienating their customers with very rigid responses to opportunities for negotiating paying back accounts and limit rate changes to increases only. Even being one day late merits a hefty payment over and above the interest finance charges. To their credit and yours, some will accept payments directly from your checking account.

Figure 11.2 briefly illustrates many of the financial terms used so far in this chapter. The third column suggests where and when these items may be used as negotiation tools. The final column is the rationale for putting yourself through all these negotiations and understanding the meaning of these terms so you can use them to your advantage.

Investment glossary.   FIGURE 11.2

TERMS	DEFINITION	NEGOTIATIONS POTENTIAL	LIFE/CAREER PLANS TIE-IN
Accrual	Accounting method where income is reported when earned, whether or not received, expenses the same	Understand the accounting system in the company you work for and especially know what method you want established for your own company.	
Annuities	An investment on which a person receives fixed payments for life or an agreed time period	Usually personally purchased from a broker. New bank legislation may allow more financial institutions to do this.	You determine with the broker how the annuity fund will be paid to you.
Assets	Items purchased with money/credit	Salary ranges, 90–120 day reviews.	Retirement planning begins.
Bank loan	Borrow money from banks on time	Interest rates, payment cycles, date to begin repayment, refinancing capability on agreed terms.	Investments in education, certification, home purchase, medical need, hardware/software as needed.
Blue-chip stock	Stock from a well-known company that makes profits, pays dividends	Often a negotiated item in addition to cash awards.	Will pay dividends as long as the stock is held and on the exchange.
Bonus	Money paid in addition to salary expected per agreement	Frequently negotiated where pay for performance is the methodology.	Learning negotiation skills on the job provides for lifelong advantages and skill building to get what you want.
Broker	Buys and sells securities	Only deal with established firms.	One method of continuous investing.
Budget	Itemized list of probable expenses and income for a time period	Budget for department needs, negotiate some home budget needs.	Good disciplined skill to have as you go toward retirement.
Capital	Wealth in the form of money or property	Cash, investments, interest, valued possessions, assets.	These continue to grow in value.
CDs	Certificate of deposit—interest guaranteed for life of the certificate	Minimum deposit and time length for deposit life.	Liquid asset when cashed.
Child care	Monies expended to care for children while parents work	Variety of options: nanny, in-house attendant, nursery school.	Know what you need and want, then negotiate accordingly.
Compound interest	Interest added to principal at the end of a predetermined compounding period: day, week, month, year	Opt for daily compounding wherever possible.	When started early, provides a great retirement nest egg.
Control	Manage the money you earn well	401(k) investment plans, pay bonus, COL increases, IRAs, stock option, promotions, SEPs.	Maintain an emergency fund of at least 10% of annual earnings.
Consumables	Items lose value over time or are depleted in volume or usefulness	Companies provide all work-related consumables.	Limit purchases that lose value over time.

(continued)

FIGURE 11.2 Continued.

TERMS	DEFINITION	NEGOTIATIONS POTENTIAL	LIFE/CAREER PLANS TIE-IN
COL	Cost of living	Some companies only reward salary increases at the COL index.	COL continues at its established levels whether you can keep up or not.
Compensation	Salary and benefits together	Negotiated as separate items. Ratio of S to B = 70/30, can be 60/40.	What you deserve is what you negotiated.
Credit	Buying on time with added interest	Emergencies, large purchase items.	Home, car, computers.
Credit card	Tool for extending purchasing power over time with interest	Travel, client entertainment, supplies needed for job completion.	Avoid using your own cards/money for job needs.
Debt	Spending more than one has earned	Assign some money to be taken out of pay before you receive it.	Reduce debt to an absolute minimum before retiring. Budget earnings against needs.
Dependents	Those whose care and livelihood are in your hands	Job placement for spouse, older child recent college graduate.	Look far enough ahead to have more money at the end of life, rather than more life at the end of the money.
Disability	Permanently or totally disabled and unable to work	Short-term and long-term disability insurance plans are available for you.	Medicaid and Medicare provide some protection in the senior years.
Dividends	Payments to stockholders from company's earned profits	Employee can purchase common/preferred stock in some cases.	Continued payments if you continue to own stock in a company.
Dollar cost averaging	Investing method that takes advantage of market swings	Investing a uniform sum at regular intervals.	$10,000 invested over 25 months could equal $12,679 (jump from $19–$23 a share dependent on market rise).
Equity	The value of a business or property beyond any mortgage or liability	Not likely, but could negotiate for some assistance given a higher cost of living than you had before the new job.	Value built in home, retirement assets, CDs, small business.
Escrow	Third party holds money without interest accruing until a deal is closed	Closing costs on a home purchase.	No income earned from this short-term arrangement, but it will be required.
Expenses	Weekly/monthly payments	Work expenses.	Budget carefully.
Futures	Professional gambling on the 90-day prediction of stock market guesses	If you have more money than you know what to do with and you are lucky, you might want to try this.	If you are good at guessing the future price of hogs, wheat, sugar, etc., continue to succeed with it. Be careful.
Home equity loans	Bundled credit card payments, education, travel, multiple residences, real estate purchases	Pay for movement of worldly goods to new city of employment, buy existing homes, refinance existing loans.	Home ownership, pay debts with one payment (watch interest rates and time factors), disciplined plans to repay accumulated debts
Interest	Charge paid for borrowing money or amount earned for loaning money	Credit may be an option where you work invest/borrow usually at lower rates.	Money earned on accounts left in IRAs, SEPs, 401(k)s comes in handy.
IRA	Individual retirement account	Deferred compensation for which you receive tax deductions.	Liquify as negotiated or according to the laws, which are subject to change.

(continued)

TERMS	DEFINITION	NEGOTIATIONS POTENTIAL	LIFE/CAREER PLANS TIE-IN
Liquidity	Assets readily converted to cash	Partial salary in identified liquid assets.	Liquifying assets as needed.
Money	Coins and securities, credit	Negotiated purchasing power	Enough money to live and die well
Mortgage	A legal pledge of property to a creditor as security for the payment of the loan or other debt	Negotiate these with bona fide mortgage bankers, negotiate for the best rates	Probably settling in on a paid-for home or deciding if you want to sell it for the $250,000+ option from Uncle Sam.
Moving expenses	Costs for moving: house-hunting, job interviews, hotel stays waiting for access to living space	Variety of options: company pays all travel costs, pays with vouchers for house-hunting expenses, closing costs. Vouchers mean you pay up front as in movers' costs.	Calculate last move before retirement, plan for buying up or down considering the current $250,000 option. Everything is negotiable so get good at it. The option may increase.
Mutual funds	Diversified investments to meet stated fund objectives	Usually a sector of the 401(k) and 403(b) investment plans.	Available as long as you may want to play.
Negotiation	Bargain with someone else to come to mutual terms or agreement	Power to determine salary, insurance, benefits, education.	Everything in life is negotiable.
Portfolio	An itemized listing of investments and securities owned by an investor	Continue to build your portfolio with diversity and depth.	Handy to have to cash in as needed.
Principal	Capital as different from revenues	Capital expenses for tools, software, membership associations.	Keep principal alive as long as possible.
Refinance	Rework mortgages and loans to prolong or shorten the term of payment	Banks and mortgage bankers to increase/decrease debt.	Refinance if it alleviates your living and buying options.
Revenues	A word for income from any source	Revenues are taxable from any source.	If income revenues remain taxable.
Salary	Systematic payment of compensation for services, work, fees.	Negotiated before work begins.	Negotiate fees for services done in return for their services to you.
Securities	Stocks or bonds, etc.	Negotiate in lieu of cash.	Probably cashing or investing further.
SEPs	Retirement plans for the self-employed	Negotiate with banks for best options.	Good nest egg if you work for yourself.
Trust	Method used in estate planning to minimize estate taxes, avoid probate, and pass assets on to heirs safely	Set up with a professional and be clear about your objectives.	Good to have established a trust even if you are not wealthy. You have possessions your heirs will inherit or the state will tax.
Voucher	A record or receipt of a business transaction	Company may agree to pay moving expenses when you submit the cost vouchers.	Any formal business transaction for which you have a written record.
401(k)	Qualified retirement plan that defers compensation to a future year	Employee and employer may contribute to this plan.	Redeemable for liquid assets after one retires or for emergencies.
$250,000 option	Capital gains exclusion on sale of primary residence	Must be primary residence for at least 2 of last 5 years before sale.	Must be 55 or over to qualify.

Taxes

Taxes are levied by federal, state, and local governments as an assessment of the cost of services provided for the common good. The application of any negotiations is not about whether you owe and must pay these taxes, but the negotiated items include things like time extension, payment of penalties after an audit, tax-deferred income, and certain tax loopholes or breaks that may apply to you. These may include child care costs, earned income credit allowances, education deductions, senior citizen care, exemptions for medical expenses, job hunt costs, and credit for each of the taxpayer's dependents.

Figure 11.3, at the end of this chapter, lists the terminology most commonly used when addressing tax issues. The second column has a commonly understood short definition for the tax terms used in this section. Ideas and suggestions for items that can be negotiated are alluded to in the third column. The final column demonstrates how these tax issues tie into one's career planning.

Filing taxes is like going to the dentist. We have to do it and wish we could avoid it. With the dentist we could end up with a toothache, but with the IRS we could end up wearing a striped suit. Reduce your tax anxiety by planning. Information you glean from these pages may even help you to save some money.

Tax planning includes the following:

- Plan your tax preparation in advance and stay on course.
- Keep all receipts and bank statements for at least 7 years.
- Keep your tax returns forever.
- Clarify the difference between a tax deduction and a tax credit.
- Each year clarify the new rules about taxes due.
- The IRS is following the rules established by Congress; the agency is not out to get you.
- IRS personnel are just people doing their job.
- You can't do much planning about the current year's deductions once you reach October, but there are other options to consider before December.
- Plan early; consult with a tax accountant or tax lawyer when in doubt.

TAX LOOPHOLES

There is a possibility of you receiving $10,000 a year from your parents, and neither of you will have to pay taxes on that amount. However, if you invest that money, you will have to pay taxes on the income earned from that investment of your parents' gift.

If you own your own home, then you are aware of the tax assessor's insatiable appetite for raising taxes in your neighborhood. These taxes can be contested, and often the homeowner wins if you can prove that your house's value has been set above the value of similar homes in the neighborhood. This takes a little work to fill out a few forms, but it may be worth a couple of hundred dollars in savings on your property tax assessment.

Itemized deductions have a potential for tax benefits. If you do not or have not itemized, you may want to consider that option. Schedule A is the tax form to itemize your deductions. The items that merit deductions include medical expenses, which the form lists so you will get all of them, taxes above and beyond what are listed on the first page of the 1040, interest expenses, charitable gifts, job hunting costs, and miscellaneous. The final figures on this Schedule A go on the appropriate line of your 1040 and will usually reduce your tax liability.

There are specific dollars for scholars. Tax benefits include the following:

- IRS 529, Post Secondary Education Benefit.

- $500 annually may be placed in Education IRA accounts. When used for qualified education purposes, it is tax-free.

- Hope Credits: $1,500 tax credit per student for 1 year. Limited to first 2-year education programs.

- Lifetime Earning Credit: 20% tax credit on first $5,000 tuition per household, not per student.

- Education IRA, Hope, and Lifetime Credits cannot be taken in the same year for one student.

- If there are three different students, then these three options could be used in one year.

- Qualified state tuition: Prepayment of tuition credits for future use, includes room and board in some states.

- Student loans, which must be repaid: You can deduct the interest for the first 6 months of repayment, up to $1,000 annually, even if you do not itemize anything else. The deduction phases out at a modified adjusted gross income of $40,000 for singles and $60,000 for joint filers.

- Roth IRAs are in after-tax money and after 5 years can be drawn without penalty for certain purposes.

DECEMBER DEADLINES

Here are three ways you can save money before December 31st arrives.

1. Where can you give money away? How much money do you have to give to others? If you ordinarily give cash, consider establishing a gift fund to help reduce your estate, which is taxed on its total value at the end of each year. Give up to $10,000 to your children so your taxable estate will be lowered. Unless your children choose to invest the money, they do not pay taxes on the gift. If they invest the money, they pay the taxes on the interest income or other profits.

2. Ask for professional tax help regarding "bunching." Bunching essentially means you arrange to pay your taxes in one year by deferring your deductions and the following year accelerating, and so on. This way you benefit from itemizing every other year while taking the standard deduction in between years. Get help to do this right.

3. Sell your losing stocks. Selling just to save taxes is foolish; however, if your stock losers are sold, they will generate a tax loss. If you repurchase the stock within 30 days, you cannot claim the loss. Buy stock in the same industry, just not the same stock.

Other tax savings from Roth IRA conversions, self-employment tax savings plans, and distributions from 401(k) and 403(b) plans will be described in Chapter 12.

Self-Employment

HOME OFFICES. Known as an audit flag for the IRS. Home office space must be used exclusively and regularly for the home business. This office must still be the primary place of business. Congress relaxed the rules in 1999 and now allows offices used for necessary management and administrative work to be considered under home office expense.

Even people who do not qualify for home office deduction may be able to deduct the cost of equipment such as computers or office furniture, used in their home offices. These articles are normally subject to complex depreciation rules, meaning the deduction is then spread over several years. As of 1999, $19,000 of such property placed in service in 1999 may be deducted, as a SEC 179 Expense, meaning you can deduct the full amount in the current year.

HEALTH INSURANCE. Self-employed people, including partners and S corporation shareholders with a stake of 2 percent or more, may deduct 45 percent of medical insurance premiums they pay for themselves and their families. This only applies to those who do not have access to any employer-paid health benefits. The deduction cannot exceed the earned income from the business. This may increase in future years. Watch Congress.

EMPLOYING YOUR CHILDREN. A child under 18 employed by parents in their unincorporated business is not subject to Social Security taxes. In reporting business income, parents can deduct wages paid the child, and the child's standard deduction will shelter the first $4,250 of wages from taxes. In essence, $4,250 of the family's income is tax-free. If the child establishes an IRA, an additional $2,000 may be tax-deferred.

RETIREMENT PLANS. Keogh tax-deferred plans must be established by December 31st of each year, but you can contribute to the plan until the tax due date. The most popular Keogh plan provides maximum savings accruing to $30,000 or 15 percent of net self-income up to $160,000. Those who fail to establish a Keogh plan before December 31st still have the option of setting up a tax-deferred SIMPLE, which has replaced the earlier SEP. Employees may contribute up to $6,000 per year, and the employer may contribute up to 3 percent of the employee's salary. The earlier SEP is no longer available for new accounts.

Independent Contractors

The IRS has set up standards to determine the classification of a contract worker including the following:

- To what degree does the recipient direct the contractor? (The more direction, the more likely to be an employee.)

- On what condition is the contractor fired? (Independent contractors should not be fired?)

- What are the legal obligations of the contractor? (Independent workers may incur civil liabilities.)

- Are assistants subject to control by the employer? (Assistants belong to the independent contractor, not to the employer.)

- Is the worker paid for time intervals? (Independent contractors are usually paid per job.)

- Does the employer provide training? (Independent contractors should possess the skills already.)

- Is the worker distinguished from the employer's regular employees? (Contractor does not do everyday operational duties.)

- Is the work performed characterized by personal service? (Contract stipulates exactly who should do the work.)

- Does the worker provide continuous service to the employer? (Services performed regularly may indicate an employer-employee relationship.)

- Are scheduling hours set by the employer? (Scheduling work by the employer indicates an employer-employee relationship.)

- Does the employer furnish tools? (Independent contractor supplies own tools.)

- Is the work performed at the employer's place of business? (Separate place of business is one characteristic of an independent contractor.)

- Has the contractor made significant investment in owned business? (A business has assets, such as facilities, equipment, supplies.)

- Is the contractor required to submit regular reports? (Regular reporting by contractors is a sign of control.)

- Does the contractor devote full time to one employer? (Contractors have multiple clients.)

- Does the employer suggest the order or sequence of work to be done? (Employer does not direct contractor about how, only about the output contracted.)

- Does the employer pay travel and business expenses? (Cost of expenses is normally covered in the contract.)

- Is the contractor exposed to normal profit and loss risks associated with business operations? (If there is evidence that a contractor suffers losses and incurs profits from the accomplishment of contracted work, then he or she is considered in business.)

- Does the contractor provide services to the general public? (Contractor may not provide exclusive work for one employer, lest the contractor be considered an employee of the employer.)

- Does the contractor provide services to more than one employer? (Contracts may not restrict workers from offering services to other employers.)

Figure 11.3 offers a chart of the terminology used in this section of Chapter 11.

FIGURE 11.3   Tax glossary.

TERMS	DEFINITIONS	NEGOTIATIONS APPLICATION	CAREER PLANNING TIE-IN
Adoption credit	Costs of adopting a child under 18 Up to $5,000 can be claimed.	Taxes owed or paid as a tax liability	Balance family and costs of adoption.
Annuity	An investment on which a person receives fixed payments for life or an agreed time period	Usually personally purchased from a broker. New bank legislation may allow more financial institutions to do this.	You determine with the broker how the annuity fund will be paid to you.
Assets	Valued and owned by you	Money coming to you in the future	Deferred income, loan notes owed
Audit	Formal examination of finances	IRS performs this service if there are questions about your 1040.	Keep all records for 7 years, all tax returns forever.
Capital gains	Percentages change by legislation. Watch the Congress, state legislatures, and local governing bodies	$250K advantage if you live in a residence for an aggregate of 2 of 5 years before you sell the home, may claim an exclusion tax	Single persons can avoid up to $250K gain and couples who file can avoid up to $500K gain. jointly
Child care costs	Reduce tax liability	Credit increases 21–30% if income is under $2,400 annually.	Need name and tax ID of person performing the care.
Compensation	Salary and benefits together	Negotiated as separate items. Ratio usually 70S to 30B, but could be 60/40.	What you deserve is what you negotiate.
Credit	Reduces tax dollar for dollar	Can usually be negotiated for cash	Continues to apply to seniors.
Deductions	Payments or taxes that can be subtracted from the total	Determined by law and time.	
Deferred tax	Payments are reserved tax-free, until after retirement	401(k)/403(b) options, pretax payment tax-sheltered annuities.	Tax liability is lower after retirement.
Dependents	Those who are partially or wholly in your care	Job placement fees, trailing spouse placement/arrangements.	Companies are willing to do this to keep marriages together and good employees happy.
Earned income	Money paid for services contracted	The money is taxable.	Congress currently talking about taxing Social Security benefits.
Earned income credit	Payment by IRS for some taxpayers	Can be applied toward taxes owed or taxes paid.	
Elderly/ disabled	Tax credit for people who are permanently or totally disabled	Negotiate short-term and long-term insurance coverage.	Age 65 or over with little or no Social Security or retirement funds.
Exemptions	Deductions allowed by law from the payer's ordinary tax obligations	Medical expenses, education, job hunt, number of children, spouse, care of related adults, blind.	Continues as long as there is earned income.
FICA	15% of annual pay goes to Social Security fund.	You and the employer split the tax. 10 quarters need to be taxed to receive maximum Social Security benefits.	Coming back to you at a rate based on your latest employment earnings when retired.

(continued)

Continued.   **FIGURE 11.3**

TERMS	DEFINITIONS	NEGOTIATIONS APPLICATION	CAREER PLANNING TIE-IN
Foreign tax credit	Foreign income or income due to temporary living in another country	Fill out all the forms accurately.	Avoid paying taxes in both countries. Seek help.
Homeowner	Mortgage interest and property taxes paid on a home are normally deductions itemized on Form 1040	Sometimes closing costs, moving costs, interest on the debt for x years.	Mortgage interest saves money that would otherwise be paid in taxes.
Hope Scholarship	Credit for tuition and related expenses for first 2 years of post-secondary education	Max credit = $1,500 per student per year.	Began in 1998.
Independent contractor	A person who works for others, has own tools, needs no training or supervision	Negotiate a contract and when the job is completed invoice their customers.	One may continue to be an independent contractor but at will rather than on a full-time basis.
IRS	Internal Revenue Service—federal government tax collectors	Pay taxes on time and file correct forms.	Seek advice if you need it, rather than risk an audit.
Liability	Legal responsibility to fulfill your tax obligation	Know what you're responsible for paying—amounts, time, forms.	Tax liability is usually less after retirement if income is reduced.
Lifelong learning	Tax credit for tuition and related expenses if needed to improve job-related skills	20% credit for $5,000 qualified expense.	Cannot be used for any year that funds are withdrawn from an Education IRA.
Mortgage interest	Tax credit for annual amount of paid mortgage interest	The mortgager will send you this accounting for your files.	As long as you live in your home or own it, until it is completely paid.
Property taxes	Taxes on property owned by you: car, boat, second home	Property taxes are figured annually until or unless you sell the property.	When you sell property, there will be a capital gains tax and sales tax.
Self-employed	Earning a living directly from one's own business or profession	Independent contractor/services.	Can build into a retirement business overall.
Shareholders	Mutual funds investors who purchase shares of a fund.	Share represents ownership in the fund's companies, pays dividends.	Can last a long time if negotiated carefully.
Taxes	Federal, state, and local government assessment of cost of services for the common good.	Time/amounts withdrawn for taxes owed in a given year or quarter.	Taxes reduced if income is reduced after age 62.
Ten forty (1040)	Federal form for filing annual taxes	Late payments permissible for cause, file right forms.	Earned income over exemptions and deductions for the year.
Who pays?	Anyone who has earned income over $6,950 in 1998. Watch changes!	W-4 forms signed with employer for exemptions.	Taxes are reduced due to higher standard deductions for people who are married and over 65.
	Self-employed earning above $400/yr	File a tax return.	File a tax return.
W-4 forms	Tells employer how much to withhold from your paycheck on your behalf	The employer is the tax collector for most of us.	Keep in mind if you are continuing to earn income through services.

Continuing Research

Light reading, anyone?

Books

Black, Richard. *The Complete Family Guide to College Financial Aid*. Toronto: Perigee. 1995.

Davis, Kristin. *Financing College*. New York: Kiplinger Books. 1998.

Detweiler, Gerri. *The Ultimate Credit Handbook*. Philadelphia: Plume. 1997.

Koenig, Harry and Bob LaFay. *Save a Fortune on Your Homeowner's Property Tax*. Dearborn: Dearborn Financial Publishing Inc. 1999.

Quinn, Jane Bryant. "Chapter Ten: Kicking the Credit Card Habit: Learning to Live without Consumer Debt." *Making the Most of Your Money*. New York: Simon & Schuster. 1997.

Slott, Ed. *Your Tax Questions Answered: A CPA with over Twenty Years Experience Answers Your Questions*. Boston: Plymouth. 1998.

Weigold, C. Frederic. *The Wall Street Journal Lifetime Guide to Money*. New York: Hyperion. 1997.

Journals

HRM Update. Pittsburgh: SMC Business Councils. 1999. (Monthly issues)

Try these sites

Money Information Links

www.kiplinger.com
(Access: *Kiplinger's Magazine*. "Departments")

www.bankrate.com
(Access: loans, credit cards, mortgages)

www.ramresearch.com
(About credit cards—more than you ever wanted to know)

www.moneycentral.msn.com
(Excellent "family financing" section)

www.rightonthemoney.org
(Everyday money issues with references to other sites)

www.collegeboard.com
(Gold mine for help making the transition from high school to college)

www.ed.gov
(U.S. Department of Education)

www.fraud.org

   (National Fraud Information Center)

www.ftc.gov

   (The Federal Trade Commission's clearinghouse for fraud information)

www.irs.ustreas.gov

   (Often a helpful site for taxpayers, despite the griping people do about taxes and the IRS)

CHAPTER 12

401(k)s and Other Investment Options

The current economy, the possibility of having a long life, the potential of living that long life in good health, plus a host of other opportunities impel today's worker, no matter how young, to formulate retirement plans that are going to serve identified needs. This means essentially getting your earned money to continue to work for you after you have received it. If your money works while you work, there are many sources of income for retirement dreams and visions.

Today's economy and the various planning options with a wide variety of companies hold a promising future for retirement planning and development. The government has made it possible for individuals to save for retirement with IRAs (individual retirement accounts), improved tax benefits, student loans, grants in aid, and military and civilian education benefits.

For years companies have offered pension plans, which have fallen into disrepute as new owners renegotiate old contracts and take some of the workers' previously negotiated benefits out of the pool. Company owners and decision makers seem to have forgotten that those benefits were chosen in lieu of paying the employees earned salaries because the company didn't have sufficient capital to pay workers' full salaries.

Now the 401(k) and 403(b) seem to be the retirement plans of choice. They offer a wide variety of options and plans, but the employee is really in charge of their contributions to their own retirement benefits. Often companies will donate a small percentage to these plans, which becomes the employee's money after the established vesting period. 401(k) is for business retirement plans. 403(b) is for those employees of nonprofit organizations to provide a method of retirement savings.

IRAs come in all shapes and sizes. These include the traditional IRA, the Roth IRA, the Education IRA, Keogh, SEP, and SIMPLE. Other tax-deferred plans, such as annuities, are available for the individual employee who works alone, in a small company, or for a giant corporation. There is a retirement savings plan for almost everyone who wants to save. There are also ways that retirement plans are portable to new companies without charge or loss to the one transporting the accumulated savings.

When you retire, you may not have an immediate need for withdrawing from the funds. There are regulations that allow you to withdraw your savings as you desire. If you are retired and over $70\frac{1}{2}$ years old, the current rules say you must begin withdrawing your money from your retirement accounts. If you are $70\frac{1}{2}$ and still working, you may continue to invest in your retirement savings plan. Once withdrawn from the tax-deferred account, your savings can be reinvested, but it must be drawn over a period of 5 years from your tax-deferred accounts. At that time you will pay taxes on this earned income.

401(k) Plans

For purposes of clarity, what is said about a 401(k) can be said about a 403(b) with a few exceptions. We'll start with the 401(k) plan because they are so pervasive in the economics of the country today. It is estimated that the amount of money invested in company-defined contribution plans has grown from $592 billion in 1988 to $1.8 trillion in 1998. This information was one of the highlights of the Morgan Stanley Dean Witter survey in the spring of 1999. The survey included 400 corporate sponsors with 1.7 million plan participants. (Figure 12.1 compares 401(k) plans.)

Before you make any contributions, be sure to check your plan's rules with the benefits administrator or with the summary plan description.

Before you make any contributions, be sure to check your plan's rules with the benefits administrator or with the summary plan description. Every 401(k) has one of these, and employers are required to distribute this information among their employees. To get the most out of your plan, know the twists and turns that are there, but which frequently need to be uncovered by you.

- Time your contributions. (You don't want to reach your maximum contribution before the year is complete, or you may lose part of your employer's contribution. For most that won't be a problem, but if you are earning $100,000 base, figure carefully when to deposit and how much.)

REPORT CARD ON 401(k)s

GRADE	Excellent	Average	Poor
SUPPORT			
Who pays?	You pay for investment management. Boss pays for administration.	You split administrative fees.	You pay for everything.
Trades	Internet, 800 number, 24/7 time.	Quarterly changes, phone or Net.	Once-a-year forms.
Investment fee	Some funds with very low annual expense ratios— 0.2% or better.	Expense ratios in the 1% range.	Fund expenses higher than 1.25% additional program charges.
Info/advice	Financial advisor to help select funds.	Lots of asset allocation info and portfolio-planning software in house or on line.	"Watch the video again." "Where's the book we gave you last year?"
Match funds	Boss matches first 3% of your salary, tosses in 3% of total salary, or may kick in even more.	Typical 50% on first 6% match.	What match?
Loans	You have a phone; you have a loan.	Limited borrowing provisions, formal loan application paperwork.	Why loans? Take a hardship withdrawal.
Vesting	Immediate.	20% per year/5 years.	Anything more than a 5-year wait.
Investment Choice	Brokerage account; eight-fund array; two to three lifestyle funds for the laid-back.	One fund family; eight funds.	We'll invest for you.

- Learn to love company stock. (The company may pay their contribution in stock. If your plan does not qualify as an ESOP (employee stock ownership plan), you may not be able to put your shares into other investment plans of the 401(k) when you are 55.

- Loans from your 401(k)s can bite you. (If your company is sold, the new owner can demand complete payment of your loan amount within as little as 6 months' time. Interest on 401(k) loans is not tax-deductible.)

- Federal rules allow companies to hold your funds for up to 60 days after your assets are valued. Depending on when the company does its valuation, you could have to wait as long as 1 year and 2 months.

- Seek professional advice. The company sets the rules it is willing to play by, but you can take advantage of them, if you know how or are willing to get professional help.

How does a 401(k) work?

- 401(k) is different from a regular pension because you are in control; you decide how much to save and how to invest, which of course becomes how much you get back with interest in retirement.
- Employers control pensions. The amount you get is based on your salary and years of company service. Coverage is capped at $30,681.84 annually if you retire after 65; at $19,943.28 if you retire at 60, and $13,806.84 if you retire at 55.
- In classic profit sharing plans, the profit sharing is dependent on company profits.
- Your employer's contribution to your 401(k) depends on your contribution rather than the company's profits.
- Contributions are tax-deferred and by automatic payroll deduction.
- Your contributions are not recorded as income on your annual W-2s, but they are recorded upon withdrawal at the appropriate tax rate.
- The government is willing to allow these tax-deferred accounts in order to encourage Americans to save for their own retirement.
- Social Security will be there, but it is not a cure-all for all workers. It was never intended to be the only source of retirement income. Today people are living longer than anyone anticipated who designed the original Social Security fund. People collect more in Social Security than they put into the system while working. That is a serious problem, which Congress must address soon.

In a nutshell: build a superhighway to your own retirement security by max-ing out your 401(k). Take charge by following these suggestions:

- Contribute often and early.
- Sort out your retirement goals.
- Make an investment plan that fits your budget comfortably.
- Choose carefully where you want to put your money.
- Keep the tax shelter going as long as you can.

IRAs

Individual retirement accounts come in a variety of flavors. They include the traditional IRA, the Roth IRA, and the Education IRA. IRAs are permitted to all Americans, but make sure you max out your contributions to a 401(k) first if it is a possibility for you.

TRADITIONAL IRAs. You don't pay taxes on accumulated investment earnings until withdrawal. You may contribute up to $2,000 or 100 percent of earned income (whichever is less) annually. Contributions may be tax-deductible, depending on income level and employer retirement plan status. Tax-deductible contributions are taxable upon withdrawal. You must begin to take minimum withdrawals once you reach age $70\frac{1}{2}$.

ROTH IRA. Investment earnings accumulate free of taxes. No taxes are due upon withdrawal if you meet qualifying rules. You may contribute up to $2,000 or 100 percent of earned income (whichever is less) annually. You do not have to withdraw funds at $70\frac{1}{2}$ years of age. Contributions to Roth IRAs are not tax-deductible. People above certain income levels are not eligible to contribute to a Roth IRA.

EDUCATION IRA. Accumulated income earnings are withdrawn free of taxation if withdrawals meet certain qualifications and the contributor pays for qualified higher education expenses of the IRA's designated beneficiary. If you do not exceed the income limits for eligibility, you may establish and contribute to Education IRAs for as many eligible beneficiaries as you wish. Current contribution limits are $500 per year per Education IRA beneficiary. Current contributions are not tax-deductible.

Traditional IRA eligibility factors:

- Earned income can be contributed
- Tax deductibility of contributions depends on income levels and/or employer retirement status.
- Contributors enjoy tax-deferred accumulation of investment earnings until withdrawal.

Roth IRA eligibility factors:

- Singles earning over $110,000 annually are not eligible.
- Couples earning over $160,000 annually are not eligible.
- Maximum contributions phase out for singles with adjusted gross incomes between $95,000 and $110,000.
- Maximum contributions phase out for couples with adjusted gross incomes between $150,000 and $160,000.

Education IRA eligibility factors:

- Establish accounts for benefit of students regardless whether the beneficiary is in the contributor's family or not.
- Maximum contributions phase out for singles with adjusted gross incomes between $95,000 and $110,000.
- Maximum contributions phase out for couples with adjusted gross incomes between $150,000 and $160,000.
- Singles earning over $110,000 annually are not eligible.
- Couples earning over $160,000 annually are not eligible.

Both Roth IRA and Education IRA are after-tax (nondeductible) contributions. The purpose for which you are investing in IRAs will help determine which IRA is the best one for you. Reasons to convert to a Roth IRA:

- Income level.
- How much is in your existing IRA.
- Tax bracket due to the Roth's tax-free accumulation of investment earnings.

Consult with a bank representative for more help.

And with all this, you still may want to run your potential choice by a professional so that you will be more assured that you have not hurt yourself unwittingly. The key advantage of a traditional IRA is that it grows tax-deferred until retirement. The key advantage to the Roth IRA is that there are no taxes on your investment at retirement.

Self-Employed Retirement Plans

Keogh:

- Defined-contribution Keogh is the most flexible and allows you to make decisions annually about how much you will contribute. You can skip a year if you like. Use IRS table to calculate net self-employment income to the top contribution of $24,000.
- Money-purchase defined-contribution Keogh has a $30,000 annual limit, and you may put away up to 25 percent of net self-employment income to that goal. No leeway on years to pay or not pay.
- Defined-benefit Keogh is the most demanding plan, but offers the greatest potential for a tax shelter. This plan works backward from what you want to receive in your retirement. How much must you set aside to meet your retirement income goals? In 1998 the limit was the average of your self-employment earnings during your three highest-earning years or $130,000 (whichever is less). Deadline for opening a Keogh is December 31.

SEP (simplified employment pensions):

- Hybrid between Keogh plans and regular individual retirement accounts.
- You must have self-employment income to use a SEP.
- Make sure trustee knows it is a SEP and not a garden-variety IRA, otherwise you may not be able to deposit more than $2,000.
- No annual reporting required of SEPs.
- No new accounts accepted anymore.

SIMPLE Plan:

- Savings incentive match plans for employees—simplified plan for small companies.
- Includes self-employed workers with no employees.
- You may work full-time, consult, freelance and have a SIMPLE plan.
- You may not have both SIMPLE and Keogh.
- You can put $6,000 a year in a SIMPLE IRA even if that is 100 percent of your earnings.
- SIMPLE IRA 25 percent penalty for early withdrawal (before $59\frac{1}{2}$ years) if you've been in the plan less than 2 years.
- Rollover and required distribution rules are basically the same as for regular IRAs.
- Plan must be open by October 1 for the year contribution is made.

Annuities

Annuities are a lifetime income stream—a tribute to the salesmanship of the insurance industry and all too often the gullibility of the customers. The money earned inside the investment is tax-deferred. Half the money in variable annuities today is inside other tax-deferred retirement accounts (like wearing a raincoat indoors).

Drawbacks to variable annuities:

- expensive insurance you don't need
- high fees
- a high cost at death

When variable annuities make sense:

- Contributed the maximum to 401(k) or 403(b), or self-employed, with a Keogh, SEP IRA, Simple IRA, Roth IRA.
- You are contributing the maximum to deductible and nondeductible IRAs.
- You won't need the money before age $50\frac{1}{2}$.
- You plan to contribute for at least 10 years before tapping the annuity.
- You plan to take the payout in a steady stream as retirement income.

> *Important directive for all paperwork that asks you to identify a beneficiary (e.g., insurance forms, home ownership options, bank loans, 401(k) or 403(b) forms, wills, trust funds, etc.):*
>
> Always identify a person as a beneficiary and do not roll into your "estate." If you have put the beneficiary as your "estate," the government will tax the estate first at between 55–65 percent. Then other taxing bodies will subtract another 15–20 percent. This leaves your estate with a pittance and sometimes a tax bill for your identified heirs. It is not your intentions that settle these matters, but what you have designated on paper forms.

How do annuities work?

- Variable annuity gives a choice of options.
- Fixed annuity deposits your money into insurance company's general accounts.
- Annuity is a personal pension plan with a measure of lifelong protection.
- It never pays off in a lump sum, only an agreed-on stream amount for retirement.
- There are a variety of payout plans available.

In sizing up an annuity, it is the soundness of the insurance company, not the half-point interest that matters. Consult a rating service if you plan to use annuities as part of your retirement plan. There are many vehicles whereby you can put away money for that rainy retirement day, but you must plan, implement your plan, and periodically strategize with a professional about whether you are doing yourself a service or disservice with the choices you have made. Never be afraid of changing your strategy; just make sure you are changing to a better one.

Figure 12.2 summarizes investment options.

FIGURE 12.2 Investment options.

OPTIONS	DEFINITIONS	NEGOTIATIONS POTENTIAL	FUTURE REALIZATIONS
Accounts	Money set aside after expenses to fund retirement	Amount to be determined by you.	Equal what you have invested, set goals to achieve.
Accrual	Accounting method where income is reported when earned, whether or not received, expenses the same	Understand the accounting system in the company you work for and especially know what method you want established for your own company.	Some use a hybrid of cash and accrual. Use it if it works for you.
After-tax money	No income tax due except the money earned as interest in the fund	Sometimes called take-home pay.	Politicians will promise, but taxes seem to be here to stay.
Annuity	Investments that function under special IRS rules	Sold as insurance policies.	If purchased with before-tax money, earnings accumulate tax-free, and all distributions are taxable.
Asset allocation	Pool of funds mixed to suit life-stage goals	Most employers select a mix to meet most needs—conservative, moderate, and aggressive.	This is a kind of mutual fund group.
Balanced fund	Mix both stocks and bonds in these funds.	You are balancing risk and reward with this fund, not either-or.	Balance also refers to your tolerance for risk and reward.
Brokerage firm	A company that buys and sells securities from the public	Evaluate a brokerage firm's rating before giving them your trust/money.	Continue to need their advice after retirement.
Commingled funds	Mix of investments for a corporate client to be sold privately	No sales or marketing expenses.	Management fees are lower.
Company funded plans	Pension or profit sharing plans companies designed for employees' use	Read the fine print; there is no obligation to invest this way.	If you are disciplined, you may want to manage your own IRA.
Compound growth	Divide 72 by the rate; answer equals years needed to double the principal	Compare years rather than rates because simple/compound are calculated differently.	Carefully compare rates of return and years needed for the investment to double.
Deferred tax	A 401(k) plan is a tax-deferred plan; taxes are deferred until withdrawal	Negotiate contract with employers to have funds withdrawn regularly.	Maintain control over your investing of these funds; it's your money.
Divorce	Qualified domestic retirement order received by divorced spouses	With a QDRO one can withdraw his/her portion of the fund with 10% penalty.	
DOL	Department of Labor	Protects employee rights to participate in retirement plans.	Statistical data is on line and free.
Eligibility	You must be 21 and have worked in the company 1,000 hours	Look up the state rules on this because an employee could be eligible to invest at 18 legally in these funds.	
Emerging market funds	Usually smaller companies registered on NASDAQ	Also most international funds are considered emerging markets.	
Employer match	There could be a company stipulation about when the company contribution becomes yours. Check!	The better the company treats its employees, the higher percentage it puts in for each employee.	Compare these deposit policies before working for a company which has 401(k)s but only 1% company input per employee.
ERISA	Provides reduced employer liability, expanded employee options	Check ERISA section 404(c) for more details.	Read the information provided carefully so you know what to expect from the company.

(continued)

Continued.   **FIGURE 12.2**

OPTIONS	DEFINITIONS	NEGOTIATIONS POTENTIAL	FUTURE REALIZATIONS
ESOP	Employer stock ownership plans	Company-sponsored retirement, profit sharing is one method.	No available buyer for your stock upon retirement, company must buy back your shares at price set by an independent appraiser.
Estate tax	37–65% may be charged to your estate; get professional advice	This is very complicated.	Develop a trust fund to save money for designated others.
Fixed income funds	These are bond funds; lending money to governments/corporations	Your likelihood of being repaid the loan rests with the credit worthiness of the borrower.	Values of shares rise and fall with the market; fixed income does not mean totally safe.
Forward averaging	Remove the entire fund at $59\frac{1}{2}$; pay taxes on it over five years	This can get complicated, so check your tax advisor on this.	Keep in touch with a professional advisor before you make a move.
GIC	Guaranteed investment contract	Usually offered by insurance and/or other financial companies.	Pays interest regularly over time, promise only as good as the firm.
Growth funds	Stocks that seem to have a lot of potential for growth	The smaller companies in a fund will be managed more aggressively.	Managers are pushing growth first of all.
Income tax	Tax on earnings paid to governments.	Adjusted often, watch legislatures.	Who can tell?
Inflation	ments. Rise in the cost of goods and services as registered by the CPI	Consumer price index statistics are gathered by the Bureau of Labor Statistics—DOL	Is credited with the rise and fall of interest rates.
International funds investments	Allow more diversity in your portfolio	Diversity means you can spread your money among a variety of options at home and abroad.	Riskier due to differing currencies, unfamiliar economic policies, and dissimilar politics.
Investment	Savings, monies put aside for growth	How much of what kind, invested with whom are all your choices.	Future goals may be realized if your investments have been well managed earlier.
IRA	Individual retirement account	Newest versions are ROTH IRAs and Education IRAs.	Anyone can set up Education IRAs for beneficiaries—one account per year per beneficiary.
IRS	Internal Revenue Service—federal government tax collectors	Pay taxes on time and file correct forms.	Seek advice if you need it, rather than risk an audit.
Keogh	Tax-deferred savings vehicle	Deadline to sign up for a Keogh plan is April 15.	Qualifications must be established by December 31.
Market risk	Prices fluctuate based on demand	If your investment doesn't grow enough, you will have a shortfall.	Watch the market carefully and then invest wisely.
Minimum distribution penalty	Retired and at least $70\frac{1}{2}$ years old, you must make minimum withdrawals	If you withdraw less than the minimum, you will pay a 50% penalty.	If a required minimum is $3,000 and you withdraw $1,000, you will pay $1,000 penalty on $2,000 balance.
Money market funds	Lowest risk of losing principal while also investing at a low rate	This is a good funds parking space before moving to more strategic markets, or before spending them.	A GIC is one of these stable investments, meaning you will get what you invested plus agreed-on interest.
Money mutual funds	On average 20 aggressive, moderate, and conservative funds to choose	Categories may be U.S. stocks or international stocks; large companies or small companies; long-term or short-term bonds.	The plan may charge a fee for providing this service.

(continued)

FIGURE 12.2   Continued.

OPTIONS	DEFINITIONS	NEGOTIATIONS POTENTIAL	FUTURE REALIZATIONS
Plan provider portability	Qualified plan will accept monies from other qualified plans	Your 401(k) and 403(b) will be accepted by other qualified plans.	Ultimately these funds could be contributed to a qualified fund that you would manage like an IRA.
Pretax money	If you withdraw from the plan, except by loan, you are subject to income taxes on that amount	Each fund manager and each fund have definite rules; know what they are and how they apply to you.	Tax due on withdrawal.
Prospectus	Document required by SEC, which discloses investment information	Registered representatives are required to give you a prospectus; you choose to invest in their fund.	Every new fund should present you with a prospectus.
Rollover	Taking money out of the fund and rolling it into another tax-qualified plan within 60 days of withdrawal	Keep rollover monies separate from any other IRA accounts you may have. Fund must remain pure.	Continuous activity as long as all funds are tax-qualified funds.
Self-funded plans	Employee has chief responsibility to decide investment strategy	The employee has the chief responsibility for the savings and investing decisions.	Employers may or may not contribute to these investment funds.
SEP	Simplified employee pensions	No longer available as new accounts.	SIMPLE was designed to replace SEP for new accounts.
SIMPLE	Plans available to companies of 100 or less employees	Newest retirement plan that enables small companies to provide some retirement benefit.	Usually available through local banks and the companies' fund contracts.
Social security	Social Security pays for retirement benefits for those now retired	FICA is your contribution of the 15% extracted for payment to Social Security plans for the retired.	If you are self-employed, you pay the full 15% yourself for Social Security benefits.
Tax-deferred savings	Money made in interest on your fund is also deferred until withdrawal	Pay taxes on income after one is retired. Reduces the tax burden.	This means taxes on any and all investments as well as salary.
Trustees	Appointment of outsiders to see that the fiduciary plans go well	These trustees have the responsibility to see that plan assets are used for participants' benefit.	
Vesting	Money you contribute is immediately 100% vested—it's yours to keep	There may be a waiting period of as many as 7 years before you are vested and your employer contributions are yours 100%.	Vesting time frames are different for different companies. Check out the rules where you work.
Withdrawal penalties	The IRS gives us a tax break with the plan and will penalize us if we change our minds in process	In addition to the income taxes, there is a 10% penalty on money withdrawn before you are $59\frac{1}{2}$.	Exceptions include: You take a loan, become disabled, die, or leave the job after you turn 55.
Withholding	Company will withdraw 20% at your withdrawal of funds unless you roll over funds into a qualified account	This is an IRS deduction for the tax owed; if too much has been deducted, the IRS will reimburse you.	No withholding will be charged if you transfer your fund directly and completely to another qualified account.
401(k)	401(k) is a plan created to help employees save for retirement	Your account is inside the plan, and you make investments inside your account.	401(k) is a defined contribution plan for contributing retirement savings that are defined on three levels.
403(b)	403(b) is a similar plan for nonprofit organizations and their employees	Your account is inside the plan, and you make investments inside your account.	403(b) is a defined contribution plan for contributing retirement savings that are defined on three levels.

Continuing Research

Light reading, anyone?

Books

Downing, Neil. *Maximize Your IRA*. Dearborn: Trade Books. 1998.

INVESCO Distributors, Inc.® (1999) *Smart Choice for Your IRA*. Denver, Colorado: Invesco.

Iwaske, Knute. *The 401(k) Millionaire: How I Started with Nothing and Made a Million—and You Can Too*. New York: Villard. 1999.

Jason, Julie. *You and Your 401(k)*. New York: Prentice-Hall (Fireside Books). 1997.

Marritt, Steve. *All about the New IRA—How to Cash in on the New Tax Law Changes*. Melbourne, FL: Halyard Press, Inc. 1998.

Robinson, Marc. *Managing Your 401(k)*. New York: Time-Life Books. 1997.

Rowland, Mary. *A Commonsense Guide to Your 401(k)*. New York: Bloomberg Press. 1997.

Journals

"401(K)ORNER" SOLUTIONS. *Investor's Press*, monthly column. 1999.

Franklin, Mary Beth. "Max Out on Your 401(k)." *Kiplinger's Personal Finance Magazine*. May 1999. Pages 61–70.

Miller, Theodore (editor). "How To Invest for Retirement." *Kiplinger's Personal Finance Magazine*. The Kiplinger Washington Editors. 1999.

Morrow, Rebecca (editor). *Managing 401(k) Plans*. Monthly trade publication. 1999.

Try these sites

401(k) Links

www.vanguard.com
>   (Mutual fund company)

www.troweprice.com
>   (IRS's understanding and calculation of investment programs)

www.rightonthemoney.org
>   (Commentary about planning investments)

www.psca.org
>   (Profit Sharing/401(k) Council of America)

www.ssa.gov
>   (Social Security Administration)

www.q&a@kiplinger.com

(Ask your questions; stump the experts.)

www.aarp.scudder.com

(News and views about investments)

www.quicken.webcrawler.com/retirement/RIRA/planner

(Compares the benefits and risks of Roth IRAs and traditional IRAs)

CHAPTER 13

Education as Investment

On-Line Learning

Penn State calls its on-line program *World Campus;* Ohio State University names its on-line MBA program *Without Boundaries.* Electronic courses are commonplace in most great universities today. To faculty and students alike, on-line education is much more than a convenience, although this is a big factor. Imagine participating in a class with 12 students representing 10 countries and 4 continents.

And what of traditional go-to-classes degree work in most colleges and universities? Earning a degree is the goal. If it is possible to do that in the comfort of your own home or office, on your own PC, at a time convenient to you, then take advantage of it. At this time there is little difference in the cost of that degree work, especially if you factor in parking fees, mileage, gas and oil, and an occasional speeding ticket, to say nothing of the wear and tear on your psyche getting to traditional classrooms.

Changes in Education

Problems with on-line education are difficult, but not insurmountable. Universities are struggling with intellectual property rights about who owns the on-line courses—professors, who compose and deliver them, or schools, which house the technology for their delivery. A technical problem is the question of increasing bandwidth for faster transmission power. This would add streaming video and other types of multimedia technology, which will make the on-line classes more and more interactive.

Students are not text-bound any more; they think visually. Many moons ago William Blake forewarned us of taking ideas and turning them into icons and worshipping them. We now have technology that people can worship or fear. Current technologies are but extensions of the human capability to learn. Personal contact will always be important, but technology will continue to grow and become more and more influential in our lives. Before it "roboticizes" us, we must figure out a way to become more human with its capabilities, rather than ignore or condemn its power.

Personal contact will always be important, but technology will continue to grow and become more and more influential in our lives.

The point of this chapter is to help us all understand the intrinsic value of education in our lives. The first issue is that learning is continuous. It does not stop at an earned degree or new certification. Career paths are built on educational acumen. Insight and imagination grow by leaps and bounds in tandem with educational opportunities. Although most learning programs, even your own planned reading program to improve your education, cost at least the price of the books, the cost of your time to read and assimilate the material and where possible the time to share your newfound materials with other like-minded investigators of the human condition. Then there is the academic cost surrounding the earned degrees from various universities—on line or on campus.

In addition, there are classes on line and in various computer-fortified offices in which learners can become proficient in specific skill sets as certified by the organization who delivers, tests, and endorses the accomplishment of certification. Planning an appropriate and challenging private reading program in one's field has always been a self-starter's continuing education plan. There is so much to know and learn how to do that learning is a lifetime occupation for the professional individual and anyone else who wishes to pursue learning for its own sake. This is truly a worthwhile and satisfying goal.

Already we can find colleges and universities that specialize in specific programs, which can be accessed from anywhere in the world. These offerings reduce the duplication of the more esoteric phases of learning, which colleges would like to administer but do not have sufficient demand to make them worthwhile to offer. Faculty members will also be able to specialize and offer their complete programs or specific courses to a larger group of learners, thus making the course worthwhile for the college to agree to offer.

How will I know what is a good on-line course/program? Be a caveat learner—explore the options, examine the alternatives, and make sure that the on-line learning chosen is what you want. Do exhaustive research, and once you have found what you are looking for, commit yourself to learning as much as you can in the time allotted. Those who have participated in a search like this and then have found the course they were looking for usually attest to spending 30 to 45 hours preparing for and responding to the course's ideas, professor's presentations, fellow classmates' chat room observations, and team learning.

Faculty Culture Shock

This is a cultural change, and not every faculty member can make the switch. Certainly all will not do it at the same time. Some are motivated by the newness of technological options and just migrate their old ways onto the technical frameworks, where these methodologies do not fit; you will notice that when you visit their Web page. Others are sure this new technology is the handmaiden of the devil and want no part of it—true Luddites of another age. If forced to participate, they will do a poor job, and the students lose. Those instructors who are used to "talk and chalk" methodology will have a hard time changing, if they ever do.

What has changed culturally is the technological availability of information with relative immediacy. Because of access to the World Wide Web, we have come to expect this immediacy at our fingertips. Incoming students are not only already computer literate, but also network proficient, and real technophiles. These students expect on-line learning to match their technical capabilities, challenge their learning curves, and to have all aspects of this on-line learning immediately available to them. This includes the professor.

Answering e-mail is no longer a measure of a faculty member's technical skills. Faculty will be counted on to teach on line (or with technology) just to stay current. This is not some kind of distance learning in the future decades. It is here today and students are demanding this type of access. They will go where distance learning is available.

Faculty innovators have already been in the forefront of teaching on line and developing their Web sites and communicating information over the Internet. Now the pressure is on more than ever for moderate or mainstream faculty to get with the program. The excuses these faculty members frequently utter exhibit more about their fear of change than their concerns about educational quality, being replaced by computers, students cheating, course copyrights, and confusions or misrepresentations about just what is an on-line course. These issues are important and we must watch carefully. However, they are more likely to point out faculty anxiety than world-shaking educational dissolution.

New Learning Models

When examining a course like this, look at the syllabus and measure whether this is a warmed-over version of what the professor does in an on-campus course, or is it truly a planned distance learning approach to the course material. Some schools just confiscate a professor's lecture notes or syllabus and call it an on-line course in management. The content is there, but the approach will not work as an on-line course. It is a learning experience that must be measured differently than the learning experience in a traditional campus course.

This is a collection of horrendous and fallacious assumptions of a bygone era, even for a traditional education system. There are still professors who teach with these underlying assumptions. You can see the signs in the syllabus, its outlined grading practices, opportunities for interaction in groups, work in teams, or upon meeting with the professor for advice.

The old model erroneously trumpets that the standards are fourfold for education to take place.

1. It is the faculty members' role to communicate information to the student.
2. Students are passive recipients of learning.
3. Faculty members are the experts in course content.
4. Faculty members, as experts, do all the teaching and students, as novices, do all the learning.

So what does the new model look like? It is likely to be a new model for teaching and learning.

1. Interactive on-line models will prove that the professor has acquired new skills.
2. learned the features and restrictions of new technology
3. devised ways to use these new features and avoid the restrictions
4. figured out ways to merge the new and old together where it would be advantageous for the learners

On-line minicourses are coming into the forefront of distance learning options. A good minicourse is just that: a miniversion of a regular on-line course. Minicourse components feature

1. introduction and overview that explain the features of a course
2. minilectures available on tape for students to see and comprehend how this works
3. calendar of dates and deadlines that refer to this particular course
4. explanation of how to use the private mail function for e-mail opportunities
5. links provided to high-quality URLs on the Web
6. chat room or discussion area where students can go to talk about the course learning
7. evaluation for student feedback and suggested improvements
8. line to access technical support when needed

On-line learning is not just limited to college degree attainment. A wide variety of companies provide training and testing about certification and skill sets. These are short-time learning options available on the Net from the originating company with their software and technology. These are good ways to earn credit for a minicourse, to gain certification from the provider, and to learn or improve skill sets that are currently needed for one's career. Conferences are held in specific fields in which college credit is often available for attending courses during the convention or conference set times.

Then there are executive education opportunities on line. Often these come out of college and university business schools. Some advertise topics such as management, corporate strategies, international business, or leadership. Others are cross-functional seminars and courses on competitive advantage through strategic capital allocation, linking customer satisfaction, quality measurement, financial performance, or new products management by managing the product innovation process. There are also human resources opportunities, accounting and finance courses, and marketing and sales programs that are made available for students on line. These are usually limited to executives, managers, or individuals with advanced degrees who want to specialize in some area of expertise that is needed in their workplace.

It is also possible to attend a convention or a conference on line. Your PC monitor will make people, places, and ideas about on-line topics immediately available to you. Even if you cannot physically attend the conference site, you can be there with virtual registration. All of the conference topics will be accessible to you. The e-clinics that have been arranged will come to a screen near you. Usually these conferences will mail you a list of the speakers and their short bios or a list of their qualifications and degrees. Some are even arranged so you can cover the exhibit hall and the wares of other companies. This may help your management and executive wing decide to be an exhibitor at the next conference or convention. The exhibitors are also listed in advance so you will know who is in the exhibitors' hall at the conference.

Even President Clinton is involved. He has issued an executive order that seeks to accelerate the development and use of learning technologies that employ the latest innovations, which will make training more productive and accessible. These include federal employees, on-line training, national databases, and partnerships.

Some of these conferences travel from city to city around the world, so you may be closer to attending a conference than you realize. Mailing lists abound about these conferences. Study them carefully and, again, be a caveat learner and select what would be the best option for you or the people in your department. Many conventioneers now offer discounts for more than one participant from the same company. Get on mailing lists and receive e-mail options for on-line learning: **www.lakewoodconferences.com** and **www.onlineworld99.com.**

Education will always be important and will always be available in a variety of options. Take advantage and keep your mind sharp both about your career and job and after retirement. Education has always been an investment, and it is even more so today. Education is one of those things that when you have it no one can take it away from you, but you can lose it through neglect. So stay sharp and continue learning all your life.

> *Education will always be important and will always be available in a variety of options.*

Psychologists have argued for at least 50 years that students are active constructors of their own learning. They are not passive recipients of someone else's knowledge that is not to be questioned or expanded in any way by student input. When you read this on the page, it sounds like an intellectual prison to be captive of one person's learning. It is.

Then what is different about on-line learning? These learners are encouraged to take part in debate about topics presented, to research opinions other than their own to augment their discussion advantage, and to become active learners. If faculty involvement and direction facilitate the discussion, the students' discussion and group activity will produce more honest learning rather than deteriorating into a gabfest or gripe session.

On-line learning requires a reconceptualization of the course content in order to effect good teaching and learning. Students will be better served if faculty change and rethink the following:

- purposefully design experiences and activities that will facilitate student learning

- support and encourage students to become active in their own learning and knowledge construction
- guide the process carefully, while encouraging student initiatives for learning new material; even information and processes the professor did not assign
- teach, as well as learn from, the students, who have an accumulated knowledge base that will help us become more informed and better instructors in the long run

FIGURE 13.1   Present and future education as an investment.

TERMS	DEFINITIONS	DURING CAREER LIFE	DURING RETIREMENT
Campus course	Traditional learning model where all education took place on a campus	Weekend colleges and distance learning options have showed realistic alternatives to tradition.	No more trips to college campuses, fighting for parking space, walking miles to class; turn on the PC.
Career university	Develop customized and flexible learning models for careerists and specialists	Focus on one's certifications, modular degrees, and skills sets accomplishments.	Open to all who can navigate the contemporary on-line education.
Case studies	Samples or examples of successful companies or operations	Learning from seeing others is available on line with ease today.	Multiple cases will be available to anyone who wants to know how a given process worked.
Caveat learner	One who searches diligently for the most comprehensive learning available	Today this means an exhaustive search to discern the real education options from frauds.	It is worth the time it takes to find what you really want to learn on line.
Certification	Process that identifies the recipient as knowledgeable and capable of practicing in a given field	More and more companies will require certification from higher and more sophisticated institutions.	No time like the present to become good at something you want to do.
College costs	Unfortunately the cost of on-line education is as expensive or more than traditional education	This could improve with economies of scale and new technologies. Diverse payment plans are needed.	Consider an educational investment like you consider your car an investment; buy a new one every 3–4 years.
Commun-ication	Academic communication has always had an aura of elitism	Technology is a great leveler in this milieu of education and culture.	New technologies make education an experience all can enjoy.
Degree	Traditional way for a student to be recognized as completing a term of study in a given discipline	Will still be awarded by college institutions, but the process of learning is severely altered.	Completion of prior learning can be extended to a degree even more with advanced technologies.
Distance education	Gaining a degree or skill sets on line	Independence ethic, self-motivated 10 hrs/week commitment, traditional academic skills.	Appeals to the home- and office bound, for whatever reasons.
Faculty	Familiar teaching modes will expand to more specialization	Courses will be chosen for the expertise of the faculty, rather than credits secured.	More variety and options available to all.
GRE	Graduate record exams	Require passing this exam before admission to some campus programs and some on-line institutions.	Can be taken at any age and in any field. Reviews available in most programs.
Higher education	Traditionally, higher education meant advanced degrees and certificates above and beyond high school	Higher education still means progressive pursuit of degrees and certificates, but technologically is more accessible to everyone.	You will be 75, but you could go to school and be a doctor at 75; continuing education is now always an option.
Interactive learning	Learning exchanges between people now made easier with technology	Interactive communication with students, teachers, and the media.	You can interact in any language, go any place, and learn what you want.
Internet	Easily available over telephone lines with on-line services	Fast learning with technology and access to remote knowledge sites.	This technology can only become more potent with wider bandwidths.

(continued)

Continued. **FIGURE 13.1**

TERMS	DEFINITIONS	DURING CAREER LIFE	DURING RETIREMENT
JAVA	Object-oriented programming language used in much of today's learning software packages	You don't need to program in JAVA in order to succeed in using those programs that have been developed.	Learning to use software without having to understand the inner workings is a current blessing.
Learning formats	This refers to the ways people learn as well as the ways people teach	Learning formats are expanding to include contemporary technologies.	If you haven't been to a formal class or in an interactive chat room, you are in for a surprise.
Learning labs	Places where interactive learning is set up technologically	Advance opportunities to meet and chat with people around the world.	Superior learning opportunities for the asking anywhere in the world.
Learning management	Using teaching and learning software systems linked to administration systems	Make use of much more technology to assist learning on-line and on-campus options.	Require some familiarity with contemporary technological systems.
Live chat rooms	Technological way to communicate with others	Improve your language skills before going on line.	Open to anyone at any time of the day or night.
Luddite	Ned Ludd of Leicestershire, England was a feebleminded man who smashed two technical frames that belonged to his employer	A group of workers in 19th century England who smashed new labor-saving technology to protest the ensuing reduced wages and unemployment.	Ned was crazy in 1779, but the Luddite movement from 1811–1816 staunchly rejected technical ways to make work easier and more productive.
Multimedia	Combination of several media	These may include TV, video, sound.	The more media used, the better.
On-campus education	Traditional education where you go to class and libraries to learn and meet other course requirements	These will continue to exist but are already morphing into weekend opportunities and Internet options.	We still look to the wonders of education in renaissance periods.
On-line education	Contemporary and future education model where access to information will rely on technology	Requirements: Internet service, software skills, hardware capability, modem speed, e-mail.	Makes education available more easily and to more people on line.
On-line minicourse	Course designed usually for acquiring skill sets or certification	Currently available in many locations.	A quick course on tax law, computer operations.
On-line student	Learning from your home or office while working from your PC	Really makes learning easy, access available, but the distractions can be ominous.	If one is homebound, this is a good option to getting a degree, certificate, or a new skill set.
On-line university	University that makes all of its offerings available on line.	In some cases there are no actual set of college buildings.	This makes the world your college of choice.
Student loan	Government programs and grants-in-aid options abound in the country	See options in Chapters 11 and 12 for some guidance here.	Very good opportunities for senior citizens in college halls today.
Television	Courses are currently available on public television or videotapes	Able to receive channel, rent lecture tapes, video programs, lab manuals, on-campus tests, reviews.	Often a good way to begin interactive learning options.
Tools	Tools for teaching and learning will be as portable as pencil and paper were in prior generations	The barriers for effective virtual learning will fall.	Robots in the form of personal assistants will enable us to learn more quickly and surely.
Tuition	Cost ascribed to a given college course based on credit hours	At the present this is true for on-line learning options also.	Some colleges do not charge tuition for senior citizens attending class.
Web sites	Creative and imaginative sites where access to information options and material are admitted by links	Most surprising and far reaching of the technological surprises for use of students and instructors.	Can only improve. Keep changing your site to match your learning.
Weekend college	Highly compacted course material in a short space of time; very intense for faculty and students	Good way for people to gain education, college degrees, and certification when they work full-time.	The pace is fast and furious. Not recommended to those who are not driven to complete the courses.

Continuing Research

Light reading, anyone?

Books

Leonard, Robin and Shae Irving. *Take Control of Your Student Loans*, 2/e. **www.nolo.com** 2000.

Stockwell, Anne. *The Guerilla Guide to Mastering Student Loan Debt*. New York: HarperCollins. 1997.

Journals

Applebome, Peter. "Distance Learning: Education.com" *New York Times: Technology*, April 4, 1999.

Boettcher, Judith V. "21st Century Teaching and Learning Patterns: What Will We See?" *Syllabus*. June, 1999. Pages 18–19.

Mendels, Pamela. "Copyright Law Raises Questions for Distance Education." *New York Times, Technology/Cybertimes*. February 10, 1999.

___. "Textbook Publisher Plans Online University." *New York Times: Technology/Cybertimes*. June 2, 1999.

Try these sites

Education Links

www.lakewoodconferences.com

(Conference education options)

www.biz.colostate.edu/homer

(Videotaped lectures/Internet discussion groups—nationally recognized MBA, $14–15K)

www.mbawb.cob.obiou.edu

(MBA aimed at entrepreneurs and innovators. $30,000 fee includes a laptop computer and room and board for three 1-week and three weekend residencies.)

www.bus.umich.edu/execed

(Executive education on line)

www.misu.nodak.edu/conted/online.htm

(Advice and counsel about what it means to be an on-line college student)

CHAPTER 14

Retirement

History

In the beginning there were not very many old people except Methuselah. In the Stone Age, most people were active until they were 20, by which time nearly all died of natural causes. If anyone lived long enough to have developed crow's-feet, being worshipped or eaten was a sign of respect. In Biblical times there were elders who managed to live a longer life than most of the tribe. When the head of the family could no longer drive a herd, feed the cattle, look for new pastures, or find new wives, he would turn to prophesying and ordering his family members to behave in certain ways.

But slowly and surely the elder population increased. By the Middle Ages, elders were a critical mass. Because they tended to hang on to their fortunes and lands, they became very unpopular with their middle-aged sons, who were anxious to become patriarchs in their own right. Even as late as the 18th century, there are plots and killings of kings and patriarchs so that sons could inherit and divide their wealth. English novelist Anthony Trollope exposed his own views of dealing with the elderly. His vision was to have all older people retire to a safe colony where they could spend a year in contemplation and then be chloroformed.

Colonial America had its prophet of gloom and doom in Cotton Mather, who advocated forcing the elderly to retire, a basic dismissal of the elderly. This did not go over very well. In the 19th century, Chancellor Otto von Bismarck of Germany had a problem with the Marxists who were trying to take over Europe. Penicillin was not available as yet, and being a clever man, Bismarck announced he would pay a pension to any nonworking German over age 65. Although this unwittingly set the world standard for retirement, Bismarck did co-opt the Marxists. In addition he established a precedent that government should help people by paying them when they are growing old.

In 1905 William Osler, in his valedictory address from Johns Hopkins University, proclaimed that the best work a man does is between the ages of 25 and 40; he considered workers between 40 and 60 merely uncreative and therefore barely tolerable. He thought the average worker over 60 was useless and should be put out to pasture. Industrialized America had little patience with older workers who were wandering around during the Industrial Revolution, dropping things, slowing down progress, taking too many sick days, and usurping the places that younger workers could occupy. This unemployment of the young was one of the causes of the 1930s depression, but the old guys would not go quietly. In 1935 President Franklin Delano Roosevelt proposed the Social Security Act, which made workers pay for their own retirement, in effect.

Then retirement hit America big time. If people were not going to work and they were reasonably healthy, what were they to do all day? Most retired people wished they could work again. Even with World War II and all the employment it brought, it wasn't until 1951 that the Corning company convened a retirement conference. One of the conclusions was that Americans did not have the capacity to be idle.

The leisure class began to develop in Florida by 1910 and work turned into play. Retirement communities were placed so that one was not confronted with the reality of seeing younger people. Segregating the elderly from active life in America worked fairly well. With the increase of golf, technology, movies, and recreation, retirement became the work of the well-to-do elderly by 1955. It was in that year that the title "senior citizen" was coined. It was meant to be a sign of respect, but most heard it as an odious and pompous utterance of the younger generations.

In 1999, the American Association of Retired Persons, once considered a great haven for retired people, dropped the word "retired" from its name. The new appellation is American Association of R****** Persons. Now it looks like a slang vulgarism on paper. This came about because a good number of the members are not retired and the coming baby boomers refuse to be categorized in that classification altogether.

In a statistical analysis, Harry S. Dixie, Jr., and James V. Smith, Jr., noticed a peculiar statistical phenomenon when there were enough years available in which this could be calculated. Adjusting for inflation, they discovered that from 1920 until 2040 there appears a high correlation between the adjusted-for-inflation stock market and the number of people ages 47–49, which they identified as peak spending years for Americans. U.S. citizens appear to spend increasingly until they are in their late 40s and then they start to spend less and begin saving for retirement. "Every 7 seconds, someone turns 47-48-49."

What Do "Seniors" Do?

Chambers of Commerce in most major cities provide assistance by way of teaching good business practices to those who want to start their own business in order to have something to retire to when they retire from their day jobs. The Small Business Administration provides loans to those who want to start their own business. The Senior Corps of Retired Executives (SCORE) provides practical guidance to individuals who want to start and run their own business. These men and women have all been in business and want to help others to do likewise. Senior citizens make up a good-sized core of home businesses. Often the business is related to what they had been doing while working for someone else, but not always.

The group *Aging with Dignity* is developing a way for retirees to tell their family and friends how they wish to be cared for toward the end of their life. This advocacy group, in conjunction with the American Bar Association, has prepared "living wills." These allow the retiree to indicate what kind of, and to what extent, medical care and intervention they want in their last illness, should they be unable to communicate that at the time. This is available free over the Internet and includes templates for several kinds of living wills that conform to the laws in 33 states and the District of Columbia: **www.agingwithdignity.org.**

Many are staying on the job. These retirees want to, and intend to, continue contributing to their communities. Far from being a burden, which is always their fear, they have become a largely untapped rich resource for all of us to use. The Committee for Economic Development (CED) issued a "wake-up call" to employers to lower job barriers for older workers. There is a national effort to combat age discrimination and provide increased training for older workers, if they wish to continue working. Older citizens seem to be enjoying their status a bit more, especially if they are healthy.

The Committee for Economic Development (CED) issued a "wake-up call" to employers to lower job barriers for older workers.

Baby boomers (those born after World War II—1960) grew up in suburban idyll. Many of them dropped out of society. Others tuned in or sat in to have their positions understood. The liberation of women from housewifery was a big accomplishment for them. They also separated sex from marriage and music from dancing. They are essentially annoying to other generations because they are preachy and self-indulgent. Most are well schooled; 76 percent graduated from high school. What they feared growing up was a nuclear holocaust. They witnessed President Kennedy's assassination and the Vietnam conflict. Famous boomers include President Clinton, Ben and Jerry, and Spike Lee.

What will they live on in retirement? Surveys show they expect to have their main income during retirement come from Social Security (32%), company pensions (20%), 401(k) (30%), and personal savings and investments (28%). What they owe at this time is credit card debt (62%). Several say they save for retirement, and the average age they began was 31. Seventy-four percent plan to work in retirement if they are healthy.

Now what about the Gen-Xers? These people were born between 1961 and 1981. They missed the 60s. Childhood was TV, latchkeys, and divorce. Their unifying force seems to have been their lousy jobs and having to live at home as an adult. They are better schooled, at 82 percent graduation from high school, than their parents. Other generations find them cynical, pragmatic, and fond of irony. There are no outstanding forming events in their years. This could make some of them bitter. Without any major wars to fight, they have *The Battle of the Network Stars.* Famous Gen-Xers are Matthew Broderick and Janeane Garofalo.

Other generations find Gen-Xers cynical, pragmatic, and fond of irony.

How do they plan to fund their retirement? Fifteen percent Social Security, 9 percent company pensions, 34 percent 401(k), and 41 percent of personal savings and investments. They also boast of a 62 percent credit card debt. Fifty-two percent say they are saving for retirement. The average age they started to save is 23. Sixty-eight percent of them plan to work in retirement (Natalia Mehlman, *Fortune.* August 16, 1999, pp. 85, 86).

Given today's medical miracles and the gospel of taking care of one's health with good diets and exercise, we are likely to live a long time after we quit work. Can we afford to retire? This is a question all must face and plan judiciously to answer. You do not have to leave a huge estate to your offspring; they can fend for themselves. But you do need enough to maintain the lifestyle to which you have grown accustomed. Some professionals who have saved enough in their high earning years retire early and do something they find more fulfilling and relaxing for less money than their high-profile jobs afforded them. They say they are happy and moving at a directed pace toward their retirement plans.

Aim to have more money left over at the end of your life than more life left at the end of the money.

Living Trusts

Living trusts enable you to transfer your estate quickly upon your death, without having to go through probate. There will be no probate expenses for your family to pay. If you are married and your estate is now worth less than $1.25 million, your family may not have to pay any federal estate taxes upon your death. You will also avoid guardianship issues if you become incapacitated, so your estate will continue to proceed as you desire.

Without a living trust, your estate, however small, may go through probate, which is inconvenient, time-consuming, and costly. Your family will have to pay probate costs, which can be considerable, thereby reducing your estate. If you are married and your estate is now valued more than $650,000 net, your family may owe federal estate taxes of 37 percent to 60 percent. If you become incapacitated, a guardianship can be expensive, time-consuming, and humiliating.

You can be the current trustee and beneficiary of your living trust into which you have placed all of your property, real estate, insurance, and tangible assets. This is a good option for older people who do not intend to make many changes in their assets picture and definitely for someone with a serious medical condition. With a living trust, you or your designated heir remains in charge of your estate and your wishes. Again, deal with a professional lawyer who specializes in trusts in the state in which you live. All states have different laws about trusts and wills.

The facts are

- Seventy-five percent of boomers hope to work at least part-time after retirement (Harris Poll, 7/20/98).

- This new millennium will see four-generation families as the norm (HHS, 2/18/98).

- Quality nursing homes are $200/day (Medicare and Medicaid, 4/96).

- Only 5 percent of Americans save with a Roth IRA (*Wall Street Journal,* 12/3/98).

- One boomer turns 50 every 8 seconds (Prudential Insurance Company, 1999).

So what should you do about this?

- Assess your goals and find the right investment mix to meet your goals.

- Take the benefits of tax-advantaged investment opportunities.
- Consolidate your retirement assets.
- Protect your estate.
- Make your wealth last at least for your lifetime (Prudence Insurance Company, 1999).

Use your imagination. The average 65-year-old retiree has, statistically, another 17 years to spend on the planet. So you need to create a vision of your retirement, not just how you want to live but what do you want to do in retirement. Feet up and rocker status satisfies about 2 weeks. Now that you have a vision, begin to fund for the realization of that vision. Saving will not be enough: *You need to have your money work for you while you are working and after you retire.* This is called investment. Your savings will not be enough to fund any real vision. Once in the market, think carefully, choose wisely, go slowly, and make every choice count toward your retirement. Timing the market doesn't work, so don't think you can do it. Retirement is a long-term commitment, so plan well.

Estate Planners

Really good estate planners know how to maximize an inheritance and minimize taxes. You probably don't, so don't try. Shop carefully until you find an estate planner whom you trust and who is willing to do this for you. Benjamin Franklin is credited with coining the phrase, "Nothing can be said for certain, except death and taxes." In retirement these two join hands, and then life gets complicated and the decisions are complex.

We now have what is referred to middle-aged wealth for the first time in American history. It used to be only the Rockefellers, the Carnegies, the Mellons, and the Kennedys. Today, because of the stock market rise, increased real estate purchases, a postwar boom after World War II, and the frugality of older Americans, who experienced deprivation brought on by the Great Depression, there is more to pass on to generations coming behind us.

The complexities of estate planning require

- a brain that can function like an accountant, dispassionate and focused
- a trust officer who understands the many ways money increases, with compound interest
- an insurance underwriter who can allocate your worth to your expected time of death with actuarial tables galore
- a financial planner who understands the ins and outs of today's taxes
- a stockbroker who hedges the market and urges you to buy or sell to advantage your stocks and bonds
- a lawyer who makes all of this finagling legal

If you cannot say you are all these professional people rolled into one, then start looking for an estate planner for your needs. Often a law office will have a group of related professionals working in their offices or who are held on a retainer for services to the lawyers' clients. You are looking for someone who understands tax and probate avoidance and who has a working knowledge of your assets. These might include real estate, other property, collectibles, stocks, bonds, insurance plans, securities, IRA options, 401(k), and 403(b) plans.

In addition, many estate planners will hold a law degree. Some may be certified accountants or financial planners by license. Law schools are currently beginning to accent knowledge about estate planning for lawyers. Even though there is a great demand for the expertise of the estate planner, there are few who have all the skills needed. Ask questions and find either the best-qualified professional with access and honesty to cover all those skills not held by the estate planner or a group of professionals from each of these disciplines residing in one office. Do not be intimidated by these people with advanced degrees: It is your money. Ask questions until it is clear to you what they are referring to and talking about with relation to becoming your estate planner. As in all things, "Buyer beware."

Late, Second, or Third Marriages

Some late bloomers marry into assets. Now what? Prenuptial agreements can fix most of this. However, if you did not do that, then complexity rears its head again in your planning. Don't be hurt if one or the other partner does not want to give up their financial independence. Financial independence includes trusts, property, insurance, collectibles, inherited furniture, dishes, silver, china, and heirlooms. Since one or both have been married before, there is a need for financial meetings at least annually to see where each other is on the radar screen to successful retirement. Assets that are separately owned can pass to your own children at your death as you have stipulated in your trust.

Long-Term Planning

Unfortunately, most of us are products of family decision makers who kept money matters very close to the vest. This is very sad when death is the cause of discovering what financial support one really has, or more often does not have. Full disclosure and candor are the only ways to help relationships grow and develop along the retirement path successfully.

Put all negotiations in writing, and share these missives with the concerned beneficiaries, if they are of an age to understand. Prenuptial agreements are contracts in writing. A prenuptial agreement defines the exposure and risk surrounding finances between two people. If you have a good lawyer assist you with its drawing, you will probably be asked to incorporate some long-term financial goals and objectives in the agreement. These might include how you will save money and invest money for retirement. If you have aging parents or handicapped children, decide between you what provisions need to be made for them. Some "prenups" are designed to last only a short number of years; others are written in perpetuity.

What if you do not have children or dependents? You may like to make some tuition payments for someone's education. You can do this without incurring gift taxes, and the beneficiary does not have to be your blood relative. This happens because you pay the money directly to the school and it can be used to cover tuition and books, not room and board.

The grantor retained income trust (GRIT) allows you to transfer assets to heirs during your life and minimize the gift tax. Congress has outlawed it for spouses, children, and siblings, but it can be used to benefit nonrelatives, nieces, nephews, and cousins. Another place for your investment may include building a private foundation.

As you can see, there is lots to think about when planning your retirement. Consult with a professional estate planner to get good advice and counsel about what is the best plan for you. Remember: You are in charge of your plan, so be prepared to tell the advisor what your real needs are. Counselors are not responsible for coming up with the plan—you are. The estate planner will help you understand how best to fund your retirement dreams.

Retirement glossary.   FIGURE 14.1

TERMS	DEFINITIONS	USEFULNESS	KEEP TRACK OF
Annuity	Investments that function under special IRS rules	Sold as insurance policies.	If purchased with before-tax money, earnings accumulate tax-free, and all distributions are 100% taxable.
Asset allocation	Pool of funds mixed to suit life-stage goals	Most employers select a mix to meet most needs—conservative, moderate, and aggressive.	This is a kind of mutual fund group.
Blue-chip stock	Offer consistent interest and growth	Hedge for inflation and retirement.	Watch the market and seek advice.
Bonds	Loan money to government/business	Hedge for inflation and retirement.	Watch the market and seek advice.
Business	Buy a successful business only	Use real estate professionals if buying rental property.	Ups and downs, depends on skills.
CD	Certificate of deposit—interest guaranteed for life of the certificate	Minimum deposit and time length for deposit life.	Liquid asset when cashed.
COBRA	Consolidated Omnibus Budget Reconciliation Act of 1985	Pays for continuing medical coverage between jobs.	Only if you are going from job to job and need coverage.
Collectibles	Expensive assets or those that become expensive over time	Hedge against inflation and retirement.	Know the real value of your treasure.
Commodities	High-risk investment	Have dollars to gamble in the market.	Be careful and go slowly.
Dollar cost averaging	Investing method that takes advantage of market swings	Investing a uniform sum at regular intervals.	$10,000 invested over 25 months could equal $12,679 (jump from $19–$23 a share dependent on market rise).
Emergency fund	10% of annual income or more	Emergencies.	No emergencies, ready cash.
Equities	Assets you expect to increase in value	Hedge against inflation/retirement.	Current value.
Estate planners	Most are lawyers	For planning estates; multiple skills.	Redemption of what you planned.
FSA	Financial savings account	Create cash accounts available for emergencies.	Roll over unused funds into your account.
HMO	Health maintenance organization	Select best option available to you.	Basic needs before retirement.
Inflation	Rise in the cost of goods and services as registered by the CPI	Consumer price index statistics are gathered by the Bureau of Labor Statistics—DOL.	Is credited with the rise and fall of interest rates.
Investment	Savings—monies put aside for growth	How much of what kind, invested with whom are all your choices.	Future goals may be realized if your investments have been well managed earlier.
Life insurance	Whole life or term	Provide for those who outlive you.	Sufficient coverage for lifestyle.

(continued)

FIGURE 14.1 Continued.

TERMS	DEFINITIONS	USEFULNESS	KEEP TRACK OF
Long-term disability	Protects against wage loss due to permanent or total disability	Employer-employee cash dedicated to this purpose before taking a job.	Social Security benefits after 65.
Medicaid	Health insurance for the indigent	State and federal social service adminstrative agencies handle this.	Continues after 65.
Medical insurance	Insurance for medical needs	Most plans split between employer and employee for premiums.	Adequate coverage for family needs.
Medicare	Social Security medical insurance	Also available to self-employed.	Plans available through SSA.
Methuselah	Biblical character who is said to have lived until he was 969	Reference is from Genesis 5:27.	Possible role model.
MSPs/MSAs	Medical savings plans or medical savings accounts in addition to medical insurance plans	To have cash in case of a medical emergency.	Maximize the interest.
Mutual funds	On average 20 aggressive, moderate, and conservative funds to choose	Categories may be U.S. stocks or international stocks; large companies or small companies; long-term or short-term bonds.	The plan may charge a fee for providing this service
Oil and Gas	Oil and gas ventures are risky	Very volatile, high gains, high losses.	Exploratory pursuits of gas and oil.
Partnerships	Pooled money for investment	Know your partners.	This is not a liquid asset.
Personal home	Beginning investment	Mortgage bankers/real estate brokers, neighborhood searchers.	Down payment reduces your monthly mortgage if it is large enough.
Portfolio	An itemized listing of investments and securities owned by an investor	Continue to build your portfolio with diversity and depth.	Handy to have to cash in as needed.
PPO	Preferred provider organization	Keep your individual family physician.	Basic health needs in retirement.
Raw land	Purchase empty lots	Select area with care and forethought.	Usually increase in value annually.
Refinance	Rework loans/mortgages to prolong or shorten the term of payment	Banks and mortgage bankers to increase/decrease debt.	Refinance if it alleviates your living and buying options.
Rental property	Real estate that is not your residence/home	Care and management needed.	Direct tax advantage.
Retirement	Withdraw from business or public life. Retire *to* rather than *from*.	Terms can be negotiated about time, place, length of hours.	No longer an active careerist or business employee.
Sandwich generation	Generation caring for elder parents and teenage-to-college-age progeny	Very harried people generally.	Planning so well their children will not have to take care of them.
Second home	Mountains, streams, ocean, what?	Real estate brokers/mortgage banks.	Do the things you always wanted to do.
Securities	Stocks or bonds	Negotiate in lieu of cash.	Probably cashing or investing further.
Seniors	People over 65	Considered no longer useful.	Whatever you want to do.
Short-term disability	Protection against lost wages due to illness or accident	Usually definite terms, but everything can be negotiated; return to job.	Could be 60–80% of salary reimbursement with tax relief.
SSA	Social Security Administration	Medical insurance after 65.	Keep current. Watch legislation.
Stocks	Cash investment in corporations for which you receive dividends	Buy and sell as appropriate.	Watch the market and carefully calculate when to move.
Vision insurance	Insurance for eye care and diseases	Eyes deteriorate later in life.	New procedures that may help with eldercare vision problems.
Whole life	Basic cash value life insurance	Not wise for investment option.	Life insurance policies are essentially "early death" insurance policies.
Worker's compensation	Employers carry work compensation insurance for their employees	Injured at work, worker's compensation pays, sometimes not all.	Not available after retirement.

Continuing Research

Light reading, anyone?

Books

Garner, Robert J., et al. *Ernst and Young's Retirement Planning Guide: Take Care of Your Finances Now . . . And They'll Take Care of You Later.* New York: John Wiley & Sons. 1997.

Lee, Dwight and Richard B. McKenzie. *Getting Rich in America: 8 Simple Rules for Building a Fortune and a Satisfying Life.* New York: HarperBusiness. 1999.

Journals

Joyce, Amy. "Career Track from Job to Lifework: Finding the Path." *Washington Post.* September 20, 1999. Page F09.

Roha, Ronaleen R. "How Late Bloomers Marry Assets: Mature Couples Shouldn't Be Too Quick to Give Up Financial Independence." *Kiplinger's Personal Finance Magazine.* April, 1999. Pages 115–118.

Try these sites

Retirement Links

www.aarp.scudder.com

   (Investment option with AARP)

www.tiaa-creef.org

   (Pension fund with a packed Web site about retirement)

www.ebri.org

   (Employee Benefit Research Institute)

www.agingwithdignity.com

   ("Living wills" designs)

www.etrade.com

   (Trading on line)

Conclusion

The trick is always to balance your life goals and career goals, then you will have enough money to fund your children's and your education, your planned vacations, your move into retirement, and your decisions about what you will retire "to," rather than looking back on what you have retired "from." You are a spiritual being and whatever wealth you have accumulated cannot be gathered without consideration of your personal spirituality and ethics.

Ethics comes from our backgrounds as people. The homes in which we were raised gave us certain values. These were challenged the moment we met some other youngster whose home rules were different than ours. In adolescence we challenged the rules and began building our own ethical standards to embark into adulthood.

Keeping track of all the issues raised between the covers of this book is indeed a lifetime of balancing the options and making the best choices. If your city is on a hill, it will be because you have made it so. Plan carefully and consult with as many people as will make your decision making more valid and more comfortable for your living.

Entrepreneur's Quiz

	Yes	No
1. Are you ruthless in personal assessment of strengths and weaknesses? (If you are just unhappy in your current job, look for another job.)	_____	_____
2. Do you have the personality to be an entrepreneur? (You may need to lower your standard of living for 3–5 years.)	_____	_____
3. Are you good at making quick decisions? (Opportunities will skip past you if you cannot assess their value quickly.)	_____	_____
4. Do you have great organizational skills? (More enterprises fail for bad management than for poor ideas.)	_____	_____
5. Are you willing to do everything in the new enterprise? (Contact a SCORE chapter about realities of entrepreneurship: **www.SCORE.org**.)	_____	_____
6. Do you think of "sell" as a four-letter word? (If you do, the first person you must hire is a terrific sales manager.)	_____	_____
7. Do you feel that schmoozing the customer is for lowlife salespeople? (This means long evenings, weekends, giving up free time to charm customers.)	_____	_____

	Yes	No

8. Do you want to have a one-person business only?

(If you cannot get along with others, selling them your products/services won't be any better.)

9. Are your family members behind you?

(If you had to come home daily to "Why are you doing this?" business would collapse.)

10. Would your children mind if you were hardly ever at home with them?

(Many children resent absent parents who are making money, even if it is for the family.)

11. Are you prepared for a 3–5 year wait for success?

(Slow isn't sexy, but it beats falling on your face by miles.)

12. Have you failed before in anything you really wanted to do?

(The rule is survival first, then push toward success no matter how long it takes.)

13. Are you patient with yourself, your colleagues, and your family's expectations?

(It is discouraging when you think about quitting. Consider everything. Don't give up your idea.)

SCORE YOURSELF:

+2 for every Yes, +1 for every No, Maximum score equals 23.

20–23   You have some the earmarks of an entreprenuer.

17–21   Think twice before you take the plunge. You have a 50/50 chance.

10–16   Stay where you are and enjoy your pension.

0–9   Cheer up! 200 million Americans are not entreprenuers!

Personality Inventory

Read each of the columns below and mark an X on the line preceding the top five words in each column that you feel best describes your personality most of the time. Proceed by supplying "I am . . ." or "I am a . . ." before most of the words.

RI	AP	IP	AS	CODE
_____ accomplished	_____ demonstrative	_____ tenacious	_____ courteous	_____ 04
_____ satisfied	_____ insensitive	_____ opportunistic	_____ scattered	_____ 14
_____ commanding	_____ generous	_____ dubious	_____ detailed	_____ 20
_____ confident	_____ agreeable	_____ good natured	_____ forgetful	_____ 13
_____ weak-kneed	_____ listener	_____ unpredictable	_____ free	_____ 03
_____ careful	_____ believable	_____ self-possessed	_____ seasoned	_____ 11
_____ determined	_____ convincing	_____ predictable	_____ dreamy	_____ 18
_____ diligent	_____ authentic	_____ fault finding	_____ energetic	_____ 07
_____ calm	_____ reserved	_____ nervous	_____ inexact	_____ 02
_____ compliant	_____ private	_____ impatient	_____ precise	_____ 01
_____ systematic	_____ self-assured	_____ mobile	_____ open	_____ 09
_____ moderate	_____ backward	_____ uneasy	_____ masterful	_____ 05
_____ stable	_____ self-advancing	_____ receiver	_____ principled	_____ 15
_____ even tempered	_____ delightful	_____ harmonious	_____ cold	_____ 12
_____ impatient	_____ talkative	_____ teachable	_____ methodical	_____ 17
_____ vivacious	_____ impetuous	_____ faithful	_____ tactful	_____ 16
_____ pensive	_____ thoughtful	_____ zealous	_____ tense	_____ 08
_____ offensive	_____ outgoing	_____ secure	_____ accurate	_____ 19
_____ demanding	_____ big hearted	_____ attentive	_____ focused	_____ 10
_____ circumspect	_____ unbelievable	_____ passionate	_____ obstinate	_____ 06

_____   _____   _____   _____   _____

TOTALS

Place the code form of the last column opposite and to the right of each column, covering the words of the column. Line up the horizontal lines on the code form with the horizontal lines in each column from top to bottom. Write the numbers indicated in the code column in the spaces provided. Mark only five in each column. Total each column.

Personality Sketch Clues

Once you have completed the personality sketch, select the column with the highest score. This column may be the one that best describes your personality most of the time. You may discover characteristics in all four areas. This is true of most people. What you are doing is discovering your predominant personality clues for greater insight into yourself. A look at the qualities and characteristics you possess naturally will help you formulate your marketing plan with more precision and accuracy.

Study the table on the following page. Reflect on the section where you have the most characteristics. Inspect the general tendencies and examine the positive and negative aspects of your predominant qualities. You are looking for insight into yourself, your personality, and your motivations. Do not be a mystery to yourself. Be honest. This is your life.

Summary

This personality profile, based on your own assessment, enables you to become aware of your personality. In the attitudes column are words that describe your personality. Is the result at least 80 percent to 85 percent accurate about you? The strengths and weaknesses columns describe your characteristics. They are two-edged swords. Example: Decisive people who push decision making too hard can become domineering. Detail-oriented people can become overly precise. The desires column describes what kinds of things would give you job satisfaction in the workplace.

In the overall population, between 15 percent and 20 percent are realistic introverts (RI: exacting, critical people generally), authentic power (AP: powerful, dominant people), or influential power (IP: influential and authentic people). Approximately 45 percent to 55 percent are accurate sensing (AS: constant and faithful people generally).

Looking at these data, you want to ask yourself whether this is the way you see yourself. Is this how your friends would describe you? And what do business associates and relatives see in your personality? This examination will help you understand yourself and your readiness for certain workplaces and markets. Test your insight against the ideas and suggestions of the people in your support group for additional verification.

Source: The psychological theories underlying this instrument are based on research and findings of eminent psychological theorists and clinicians as this information has been made public over the last century. The instrument design and focus are original and of proprietary interest to the author. The ideas and research used in developing this instrument find their roots in Carl Jung's personality theories, Meyers/Brigg's theories for testing personalities, Richard Bolles's personal assessment tools, Jackson's personality characteristics scales, and Charles Hampden-Turner's brain personality theories.

PERSONALITY PROFILES

	Attitudes	Strengths	Weaknesses	Desires
Sketch	"I am characterized by..."	"I am energized by..."	"My shortcomings are..."	"In a job I need..."
RI	Realism Diplomacy Organization Politics Comprehension	Detail Caution Orthodoxy Rationality Perceptiveness	Overly accurate Procrastinating Unable to delegate Fearful of job reviews	Concentration Precision Encouragement Work guidelines Clarity

My *general* tendency is to see all sides and be intuitive. I am intolerant of differing views and reject criticism.

AP	Assurance Fearlessness Self-centeredness Power Energy	Problem solving Decision making Goal setting Pioneer spirit Creativity	Indiscreet Domineering Spontaneous Fearful of others' 　opportunism	Position Authority Prominence Power Open speech

My *general* tendency is to be direct and goal oriented. I seldom listen to others and often dismiss their ideas/opinions.

IP	Cheerfulness Sociability Fluent speech Impetuous Sensuality	Inspiration Communication Performance Collaboration Assisting others	Easily persuaded Roundabout Unaware of time passing Fearful of losing social 　contacts	Status Accreditation Independence Acceptance Speak out

My *general* tendency is to respect others and be open minded. I am often too sensitive and defensive.

AS	Faithfulness Stability Leisure style Long-suffering Predictability	Concentration Individualization Cohesiveness Security Attentiveness	Retentive Convivial Assured Fearful of losing security	Stability Convention Assurances Community Acknowledgment

My *general* tendency is to listen and have balanced reactions. I avoid conflict at all costs.

Letters

Cover Letters

Cover letters have different purposes: They are target (answering an ad), broadcast (announcing your arrival in a geographical area or a new field), peer network (gaining information from future peers), and decision maker network (gaining information from people who have the authority to hire you).

A traditional block format is suggested for all these three-paragraph business letters. Content of the three paragraphs would be:

1. Explain how you came to know of the addressee and what you want.
2. Tell more about the signatory's need to meet with the addressee.
3. Enclose a résumé; identify a time when you will call to set an appointment.

Close with your traditional letter closing: Sincerely, Yours truly, or Cordially.

Make sure your sentences are complete but not too long. Keep the letter focused. You are asking someone whc is very busy to read your letter and make a decision to see you for an appointment. Busy people always appreciate it if you are concise and to the point.

Other Letters Used in a Search

A *minirésumé* or market letter is used in very specialized places: to an executive you have been unable to reach in your campaign or to someone at an elevated managerial level. This minirésumé would be used in the final stages of your campaign, after about a 6-month search. Most searchers will not need to use it at all because they will have a job before needing this letter.

The *inquiry letter* is just that, an inquiry into the company's potential job openings, geographical locations, other information. Make sure you are unable to get the information you want from doing research. Otherwise the company officials will not answer your letter and will not see you. You will be perceived as lazy or incompetent. So much information is available on the Web.

A *letter of acceptance* is good form even when you have answered yes over the phone or in person. Keep in mind all of the things you have negotiated, and summarize your understandings in a one- or two-page letter of acceptance. This letter is sometimes called a memorandum of record in legal terminology.

Withdrawing your name from consideration is something you should do formally and in writing with all those companies where you were considered seriously for a professional position. Do this after you are absolutely positive you have landed the job of your dreams.

Networking letters go to all those who gave you good advice, encouraged you in your search, gave you leads to good companies, and may have asked to be kept abreast of your progress. They want to know what happened to you, so pen a note and tell them. Some you may want to meet for lunch again.

Market Value

The Worksheets on the following pages will give you a chance to evaluate job opportunities. A sample, already filled in, is provided for each worksheet.

JOB ACCEPTANCE CRITERIA

JOB SATISFACTION VALUE *Rate on a scale of 1–10.*

Meet career objective	_____	Product and service	_____
Room for advancement	_____	Profit	_____
Challenging work	_____	Nonprofit	_____
Use developed skills	_____	Room for creativity	_____
People environment	_____	Moving expenses to negotiate	$ _____
Private workspace	_____	Moving furniture	_____
Geographic preference	_____	House-hunting trip	_____
Management style		Interviewing expenses	_____
Authoritarian	_____	Lodging/food expenses	_____
Patriarchal	_____	Spouse/child career/	
Participative	_____	school placement	_____
Laissez-faire	_____	Other potential work costs	$ _____
Product	_____	Car/travel allowance	_____
Service	_____	Expense accounts	_____

COMPENSATION $ _____

Write in dollar amounts				Vacation/time off			
Salary	$ _____	___	___	Days vacation	_____	___	___
90-day review	_____	___	___	Holidays	_____	___	___
Annual salary	_____	___	___	Sick leave	_____	___	___
Benefits	_____	___	___	Personal leave	_____	___	___
Insurance	_____	___	___	Education cap			
Major medical	$ _____	___	___	Complete degree	_____	___	___
Life rider	_____	___	___	Seminars	_____	___	___
Accident	_____	___	___	Workshops	_____	___	___
Short-term disability	_____	___	___	Conventions	_____	___	___
Long-term disability	_____	___	___	Family options	_____	___	___
Dental	_____	___	___	Other benefits			
Eye	_____	___	___	Pensions	_____	___	___
Pregnancy	_____	___	___	Bonuses	_____	___	___
Individual	_____	___	___	Stock options	_____	___	___
Family	_____	___	___	Box seats	_____	___	___
HMO	_____	___	___	Outplacement costs	_____	___	___
PPO	_____	___	___	Indigenous benefits	_____	___	___
Other	_____	___	___	Other	_____	___	___

JOB ACCEPTANCE CRITERIA SAMPLE

JOB SATISFACTION VALUE   *Rate on a scale of 1–10.*

Meet career objective	10	Product and service	10
Room for advancement	8	Profit	10
Challenging work	10	Nonprofit	0
Use developed skills	10	Room for creativity	10
People environment	8	Moving expenses to negotiate	$ 14,000
Private workspace	8	Moving furniture	4,000
Geographic preference	San Jose, Calif.	House-hunting trip	2,000
Management style		Interviewing expenses	2,000
Authoritarian		Lodging/food expenses	2,000
Patriarchal		Spouse/child career/	
Participative	10	school placement	4,000
Laissez-faire		Other potential work costs	$ 6,000
Product	5	Car/travel allowance	25¢/mi
Service	5	Expense accounts	credit card

COMPENSATION $ 34,325

Write in dollar amounts

			Vacation/time off		
Salary	$ 26,000		Days vacation	10	
90-day review	1,050		Holidays	10	
Annual salary		27,050	Sick leave	5	
Benefits		7,275	Personal leave	5	
Insurance	3,375		Education cap		3,000
Major medical	$ 1,200		Complete degree	XX	
Life rider			Seminars		
Accident	750		Workshops		
Short-term disability	750		Conventions		
Long-term disability			Family options		
Dental	125		Other benefits		400
Eye	150		Pensions		
Pregnancy	400		Bonuses	400	
Individual			Stock options		
Family	XX		Box seats		
HMO			Outplacement costs		
PPO	XX		Indigenous benefits		500
Other			Other		

MARKET VALUE DETERMINATION

To determine personal market value in a career search, investigate and evaluate the market record at that time and add your personal earnings record.

	Low	High	Average
MARKET RECORD (consider the last 6-months to 1-year time frame)			
Ads	_____	_____	_____
Agencies (include graduate placement)	_____	_____	_____
Chambers of Commerce (where you live)	_____	_____	_____
U.S. Department of Labor	_____	_____	_____
Peer interviews (about 5–6 interviews)	_____	_____	_____
Average totals	_____	_____	_____

PERSONAL EARNINGS RECORD (consider the last 6-months to 1-year time frame)

	Low	High	Average
Value of jobs held (figure at full-time)	_____	_____	_____
Calculate 25 percent benefits package (even if you do not receive benefits)	_____	_____	_____
Personal earnings total (add)	_____	_____	_____

SUMMARY

	Low	High	Average
Market record	_____	_____	_____
Personal earnings record	_____	_____	_____
Sum	_____	_____	_____
Divide sum by two	_____	_____	_____
Calculate an additional 25 percent benefit package	_____	_____	_____
Add last two numbers in columns (determines total compensation potential)	_____	_____	_____
Assess personal market range Turndown point	_____	_____	_____
Realistic potential high	_____	_____	_____

MARKET VALUE DETERMINATION SAMPLE

To determine personal market value in a career search, investigate and evaluate the market record at that time and add your personal earnings record.

MARKET RECORD (consider the last 6-months to 1-year time frame)	Low	High	Average
Ads	$22,000	$28,000	$25,000
Agencies (include graduate placement)	22,000	29,000	24,500
Chambers of Commerce (where you live)	20,000	30,000	25,000
U.S. Department of Labor	18,000	35,000	26,500
Peer interviews (about 5–6 interviews)	22,000	26,000	25,000
Average totals	$20,400	$29,600	$25,000

PERSONAL EARNINGS RECORD (consider the last 6-months to 1-year time frame)			
Value of jobs held (figure at full-time)	18,000	20,000	19,000
Calculate 25 percent benefits package	+4,500	+5,000	+4,750
(even if you do not receive benefits)			
Personal earnings total (add)	$22,500	$25,000	$23,750

SUMMARY			
Market record	20,400	29,600	25,000
Personal earnings record	+22,500	+25,000	+23,750
Sum	42,900	54,600	48,750
Divide sum by two	21,450	27,300	24,375
Calculate an additional 25 percent benefit package	+5,363	+6,825	+6,094
Add last two numbers in columns	$26,813	$34,125	$30,469
(determines total compensation potential)			

Assess personal market range   Turndown point   _____ $27,000 _____

                              Realistic potential high   _____ $34,125 _____

Procrastination

Who Are These People?

Procrastination messes up more lives and businesses. The rationale for procrastination produces a wide variety of regrets: perfection, fantasy, fear, catastrophes, anger, overdoing, and pleasure seeking, to name a few. You will notice that these few named are among the most frequently identified excuses for why something needs to be put off to another day or time. Are these activities necessary or can they be corrected?

If you are a procrastinator, examine why you do this. There could be a set of reasons, or one predominant reason that rises to the top of your self-understanding. Individuals who procrastinate sometimes set unrealistic expectations for themselves and for others. Their judgment is impaired by their overanxiousness to succeed or to please someone.

Others are detail oriented to the utmost, usually driving others crazy with their constant pursuit of the least little suggestion of error. They shower all they do with this rough assessment that the details are not as complete as they might be, so this project is not complete. These individuals never heard of the saying, "Some things just need to be done; they don't have to be perfect in every detail."

Students often suffer from putting assignments off to the last minute, only to find that it will take more time and they cannot possibly get the assignment finished on time. The excuses given to professors about what has happened are legendary and oft repeated. Time pressure will motivate some, but the error rates in those assignments are often very high and therefore negate the effort of midnight oil burning.

Watch people going down the highway just to notice how many things you see one driver doing. I am assuming you are in the passenger seat while you do this. You may notice a driver execute a near miss with an illegal left turn, go faster than others on the road, drink coffee, answer a cell phone, comb hair, put on makeup, and wave or honk to friends. And he or she does all this while driving a fast-moving missile through crowded intersections in center city areas, even past school zones. They clearly are not focused.

Some individuals let their anger get the best of them and take it out on work or project completion. This provokes others if these angry individuals are not carrying the team burden. There really is no place for anger in professional settings. If your home life or your personal life is in trouble and you cannot control your anger over the situation, seek advice and counsel to help you with this problem. You make the workplace a dangerous place for everyone to be.

Sometimes there is real fear of failure as a task is assigned to you and you really do not know how to begin, much less complete, the project. This is a time to meet and consult with someone else who can help you. Otherwise you will fritter away the time the project will take and not have it finished on time. Recognizing that we need help is a big need in some business operations.

What to Do about Procrastination

Perfectionists: If you are among this group, throw away most of your "shoulds" and "oughts." Reduce your use of the word "must" and substitute "may." Give yourself two or three deadlines to complete the project on time. The first two being according to your timetables and the third the actual date the project is due. Then if you meet either of your goals, you will have time to be "more perfect" for the final draft.

For those of you who live in cyberspace or some other fantasy dream while you are working. You need to come to Earth more often. Because you dream so much, you promise more than you, or anyone else, could do in the time suggested. Be realistic and if you need to, then please get a good friend to help you become more "this worldly." Setting up earlier deadlines, as suggested for the procrastinators among us, may help you also. Then you will have time to dream between meeting your goals and arriving at the agreed-to goals on time.

Fear is not usually considered very good; but it is good. It is fear that will give you extra adrenaline to be helpful to others in crises or accidents. Fear enables you to walk away from a fight you can't possibly win. Fear is good, but paralyzing fear is not. If you fear an assignment, examine what it is you fear will happen to you. Now judge if that is a realistic fear or just a bad fantasy you have cooked up for yourself. Only about 10 percent of all the stuff we thought could happen does, but then never in the way we thought it would. Drop your fears and be brave. Take on new tasks. Your natural fearful state will warn you early enough if something really is too much for you.

Catastrophists are really difficult to be around because they always see the worst possible scenarios to every situation. And when they tell the story, you would think the end of the world was just around the corner. As we came to and passed through the end of one millennium, I am sure you read dire consequences being prophesied by catastrophists. The fears were about not having enough water, heat, or electricity. Others felt they needed to defend themselves against neighbors with armed supplies. And still others stored vast quantities of food and supplies that would not be used in 5 years. The amazing thing is that the most fearful dug holes in the Earth and camouflaged them so no one could find them. In their hideouts they stored all of the above-identified supplies. These people are misguided militarists and need other outlets than their crisis-creating mental images.

Anger destroys on both sides of the anger. If you are angry with someone, don't take it out on your possessions. Go to the individual with whom you are angry and try to square the differences. This may not always be possible. But more is possible than is ever attempted by angry people. The best way to overcome anger is to identify its roots and if they are in you, do something about it. If it is someone else's problem, don't be sucked into it or your anger will be fueled by theirs and that is not good for anyone.

Some people just overdo. To them, everything is of the utmost importance and must be attended to immediately with all the resources available. The self-righteous schoolmarm approach of, "Well, if I don't do it, who will?" needs to go. Knowing how to prioritize and delegate fails to cross these individuals' thoughts more than once a decade. Some things are just busywork, and other things are extremely important. Most of the rest falls in the middle. So train yourself, if you are an overdoer, to measure and prioritize your projects and responsibilities so you know the difference and can make decisions without burdening yourself into oblivion. Get a life!

Pleasure seekers have little use for the "play comes after work" concept. They are into immediate gratification, and if that means delaying work on a project or assignment, they will procrastinate. The problem is that these individuals expect everyone else to assist them in meeting the deadline or to forgive them for missing it. Learn to reward yourself in other ways than slacking off on agreed-to projects or assignments. You'll make more friends and pretty soon you may enjoy your work.

These are not the sum total of people who procrastinate, but if you procrastinate, I am sure you found yourself in some of these behavioral descriptions. Try new behaviors and combat whatever it is that causes you to procrastinate. It is not a natural phenomenon that everyone suffers. So bring a little discipline and a few friends into your life to help you move along at a better pace to the finish line.

APPENDIX F

Glossary

CAREER

benefits package: Combination of benefits that have a monetary value and are 25 to 30 percent of one's total compensation. These may include bonuses, box seats, car or travel allowance, company car, credit cards, education cap and tuition reimbursement, expense accounts, identified leave, holidays, insurance, outplacement, pensions, professional control, stock options, trailing-spouse accommodations, and other items negotiated by the job candidate and the company negotiator.

candidate: Individual implementing a career search after graduation from college.

career centers: Identified separate places in libraries where career searchers can research data.

career focus: Larger career goal than that specified as career objective on the résumé.

career objective: Clearly focused goal statement of place, skill, and reason to hire that introduces the résumé.

career search: The marketing method whereby a graduate designs and implements the best and most professional way to uncover the best job opportunity available at the time.

compensation: Combination of salary plus benefits in exchange for services and skills provided to the employer.

consultants: Individuals who have specific skills that are in demand and are willing to move from company to company performing their skills.

curriculum vitae: Complete list of one's accomplishments, publications, awards, and prior employment; still used in Europe and in Japan, also for academic positions.

dream job: That position the candidate feels most completely matches his or her career objective.

earnings power: How much compensation one is able to negotiate given the market and the person's history of earning.

entrepreneur: A risk taker who believes in the ideas or projects generated and who is willing to strike out individually if necessary to work in the desired field.

four Ps: Marketing mix that is deemed successful in selling a new product or service; its elements include price, place, product, and promotion.

GAME Theory: Theory developed by John von Neumann in a book of the same name to enable people to make valid decisions among variables that are not equal but can be based within mathematical equations.

graduate placement: Offices on campuses whose role is a combination of job interview preparation, support, record keeping, and counsel to graduates of the school.

hidden market: Unlisted but existing positions; created positions make this list.

house-hunting expenses: To be negotiated by the job applicant; may include other adult decision maker and the applicant's separate or extended trip to explore the housing market. This includes travel, lodging, and food, but it must be negotiated.

HRM: Human resources management. Usually responsible for interviewing activity.

indigenous benefits: Those benefits that come because of an individual's position in the company or are made available to all employees because the products or services are natural to the company.

InfoTrac: CD-ROM package available to libraries that includes "Business Profiles" and "Magazine Files" that can be made available to searchers by topic, name, geographic area, field, or career. This information can then be printed for the searcher.

Interviews: Face-to-face communication, conversational-style, to determine information. Can be conducted for evaluation, information, job, negotiation, and style determination of a company and of a candidate. Interviews may also be conducted by electronic means today.

intrepreneur: Individual who functions as an entrepreneur but is within a company, often the head of a specific division in which the person's expertise is in demand.

job: Industrial-age icon that describes work for hire in the industrial age.

job search: Another name for career search. Can be conducted using traditional tools, contemporary networking methods, and/or electronic means available to a searcher. In-house searching is also possible for those who want to improve their positions within the company currently employing them.

keyword stripe: Line of 45 to 60 characters that highlights one's skills, degrees, and employment and is placed at the top of the résumé before the personal identification data.

knowledge workers: Individuals whose heads are valued more than their hands.

marketplace: Work environments of chosen careers.

memorandum of record: Written statement of job acceptance that includes listing of negotiated items. Candidate also asks for verification of understanding by a certain date.

minirésumé: Résumé designed as a business letter aimed at top executives; used only at the end of a campaign if the dream job is still not forthcoming.

moving expenses: Expenses to be remunerated to the candidate on submission of vouchers or some other system. These include movers' fees, stays in motels, and lodging while household goods are transported (covers candidate and all dependents). Must be negotiated; cannot be assumed.

naysayer: Individual who always sees the dark side of things.

negotiate: Process of give and take that results in a candidate and a company agreeing on terms of employment.

outplacement: Negotiated approach to placing a valued employee elsewhere because of company policy that forces the employee out of a job through no fault of that employee.

part-time worker: Individual whose services and skills are available for hire, usually through a temporary placement agency and on a short-term basis.

partnership: Private business group of individuals with similar or various backgrounds who agree to support, run, and oversee a chosen business resulting in shared profits for these partners at the end of successful years.

placement: The practice of arranging for an employee to be hired for a specific responsibility.

power lunch: 1990s name for business lunch among colleagues or professionals.

prospects: List of individuals to be seen as part of a search campaign or sales tool.

résumé: Tool to announce a candidate's readiness, preparation, and interest in a career field.

Résumé may appear in a variety of formats, but the information remains the same in all.

salary: First step in a negotiation process to assign monetary value to one's compensation with respect to candidate's accumulated skills and company needs identification.

skill: Keyword in current search campaigns. Companies are looking for and will pay for skilled people. High priority of information identified on a résumé.

sole proprietorship: Individual- or family-owned business.

succession charts: Method for identifying people, process, and method for promotion within a company structure.

technician: New definition to accommodate the knowledge worker who defines skills acquired in technical terms, thus translating for the résumé reader what is significant about how individuals use their knowledge and degree.

temporary worker: Another name for part-time worker.

trailing spouse: Current term to identify individual for whom the new employee is negotiating terms because these individuals are usually in professional positions themselves, which they have to give up for the potential employee to move and accept a position.

translator: Job searcher must be able to translate capabilities for the reader of the résumé, the interviewer for the job, and the negotiator for compensation.

wage earner: Individual who gets paid for the practice and use of his or her skills and knowledge.

10K report: Similar to an annual report but in greater depth; prepared for SEC when a company petitions to change its position on the stock exchanges.

401(k) pension plans: Pension options available for most employees in good companies.

90-day review: Opportunity to assess one's performance and receive a raise within the first year.

TECHNICAL

ADF: Automatic document feeder. Feeds documents into fax machines without operator assistance.

America Online: One of the many commercial services that provide access to the Internet.

analogue transmission: Traditional telephone technology in which sound waves or other information is converted to electronic impulses of varying lengths.

applets: Mini-programs that can be downloaded quickly and used by any computer equipped with a Java-capable browser. Applets carry their own software players.

ASCII: American standard code for information interchange. Seven-bit coding system represents data for processing and communications. Text characters are faxed over phone lines.

bit: One binary digit, either 0 or 1.

bps: Bits per second. The number of data bits sent per second between two modems; measures the rate at which the information is handled, manipulated, or transferred.

bus: The group of conductors that interconnect individual circuitry in a computer.

byte: Eight related bits of data; an 8-bit binary number.

cable modem: Connects computer to high-speed coaxial line carrying a cable TV signal into the home. Can receive data at speeds of up to 10 million bits per second (bps), about 700 times faster than the 14,000-bps modems many use today.

cache: High-speed processor memory that buffers commonly used instructions or data.

CD-ROM: Flat laser disc used to store information at greater density than floppy disks.

coaxial cable: Transmission line with a central core that conducts electricity. Coaxial cable can transmit more information than a pair of twisted copper wires, which are commonly used for telephone communication.

computer age: From about 1975 to today.

CPU: Central processing unit. The part of the computer that controls the hardware during operations.

cyberspace: Where Web sites go to be organized and made available to Internet users.

digital age: The time when analogue technology has been replaced by digital technology. Also refers to those individuals born from 1980 to the present.

digital transmission: Converts sound waves and other information into binary computer code, which is a series of zeros and ones. The binary code is converted back when it reaches its destination.

DIO: Digital input/output.

disk: A thin, flat plate inserted into a plastic cover, size $5^1/_4$ or $3^1/_2$ inches. A data disk is used to store information/data from computer operations. A demonstration disk is used to demonstrate a product or service. Computer information systems scientists design the programs for software use: word processing, spreadsheet, games, graphics, design, and so on.

DRAM: Dynamic random access memory. Volatile storage that may not be interrupted; if it is, information will be lost.

dumb terminal: A computing unit with a keyboard and screen but no internal memory; it functions as an input–display unit only.

electronic media: Means of dispersing information and data by electrons over fiber-optic cables.

e-mail: Electronic mail. Transfers text messages, memos, and reports over a network.

emoticon: Punctuation symbols typed sideways to communicate messages through e-mail :), : (.

fourth-generation language: Programming language not so heavily reliant on code as its predecessors.

Genie: Search engine for the Internet through Netscape.

gigabyte: 1 billion bytes, or 1,000 megabytes.

Gopher: Internet browsing server in which information is arranged by menus.

hardware: All the technical tools that are used in computer operations other than the software programs and databases: computer, printer, peripherals, mouse, and so forth.

home page: Display on the WWW that usually identifies and describes the page owner and contains links to other pages.

HTML: Hypertext markup language. Common language of Web documents.

http: Hypertext transfer protocol. Allows for instant, seamless transfer of information across the Web.

hypertext: Text and graphics in Web documents can be linked to text and graphics in other Web documents; they are accessed with a simple mouse click.

Internet: World's largest network, consisting of 100,000 individual networks supporting nearly 20 million computers, linking governments, universities, and commercial institutions.

ISDN: Integrated Services Digital Network. Digital network that supports high-speed transfer of fax, data, voice, and video over standard copper telephone wire at speeds of up to 128,000 bps in the digital format computers can process.

JAVA: Programming language from Sun Microsystems allowing animations, sounds, and instant updates of information.

Jughead: Tool to search specific Web site.

LAN: Local area network. Telecommunication links and networks within a local area.

LED: Light-emitting diode. An array of pixel-size lights within a stationary printhead.

Lycos: A search engine that helps you locate resources by keywords.

mainframe computer: Manages large amounts of data and complex computing tasks. Also describes memory storage and the computing part of a large computer system.

MB: megabyte. Equals 1 million bytes.

microcomputer: PC based on a single-chip processor.

microfiche: Microfilm that contains rows of pages in reduced form.

Microsoft Office: Set of software packages, Access, Excel, Mail, PowerPoint, Project, and Word, for use separately or in combination for word processing, spreadsheets, graphics, e-mail, calendars, and so forth.

minicomputer: Medium-size computer running a multitasking operating system capable of managing 100 users simultaneously.

modem: *Mo*dulate/*Dem*odulate. The sending modem converts digital data to analogue form; receiving modem converts analogue signal back to digital.

Monster Board: Popular graphical Web browser and database for job hunters; emphasis is east of the Mississippi.

Mosaic: Very popular graphical Web browser and database for job hunters; emphasis is west of the Mississippi.

multimedia: Hardware and software capable of delivering not only text but also digitized voice, image, and video presentations of information.

multitasking: Several processors can be run simultaneously.

Net: Shortened form of *Internet.*

netiquette: Proper etiquette when communicating over the Internet.

Netscape: Network browser currently replacing Mosaic.

network: Connected cables through which a variety of information, data, and messages can flow within and among organizations, regions, neighborhoods, satellites, TVs, and so forth.

newsgroup: A discussion group on a specific topic, maintained on a computer network or a bulletin board.

Newsnet: Sophisticated electronic news clipping service. Provides latest information daily. Great preparation for interviews for which you need recent company information.

object-oriented database: Database organized around an object model rather than the conventional models.

object-oriented technology: Computer programming that builds software applications through repeated use of self-contained objects—bits of data that are surrounded with the program information needed to gain access to the data. Objects can perform certain computer functions when they receive messages to do that function.

OCR: Optical character recognition. A scanning device to convert paper documents to electronic alphanumeric characters that can be stored in a computer.

PowerPoint: A graphics production software within Microsoft Office using a Windows environment.

protocol: Exact sequence of bits, characters, and control codes used to transfer data between computers and peripherals through a communications channel.

résumé: Electronic résumés include all résumés made and communicated by means of electronic disks, CD-ROMs, in ASCII text, with multimedia, videotapes, slide presentations, and over the WWW with a Web home page. They may or may not be interactive. All require a computer to decipher. Some are stand-alone disks with directions about how to access data; others require a certain standard of operating system or software packages to access the data.

software: Disks that are individually or commercially programmed for business operations using computers or personal computer operations such as games.

stand-alone program: A compiled program that runs with the operating system but without any other software programs or environments.

Telnet: Program that allows you to move all over the world and select files electronically from computers nearby or far away.

Turbo C, C++: Object-oriented programming software packages.

URL: Uniform resource locator. File name of any object that can be addressed on the Web, point on an HTML page, graphic in a directory, or even an executable script.

Usenet: A large group of networks and computers that organizes messages by newsgroup; a branch of the Internet.

user-friendly: Term used to indicate that a software package will be easy to use for the nontechnical person who needs what the program provides.

Veronica: A frequently updated index system intended to make Gopher even easier to use.

videotape: A videotaped record of information, data, slides, multimedia, and so on.

visibility: Candidates for jobs can make themselves visible to employers 24 hours a day by using the technology currently available.

Visual Basic: A fourth-generation database programming language.

voice telephone: E-mail or other mechanisms for sending and receiving messages.

WAN: Wide area network. Long-distance telecommunication links and networks that connect local area networks and end stations regionally, nationally, or internationally.

Web: Text, graphics, video, and sound used separately or in combination to produce a site or to develop a home page.

Windows: Operating system from Microsoft.

word processing: Using computers and software programs to type, arrange, correct, and improve typed copy of business or personal information and store on a floppy disk.

WWW: World Wide Web. A popular and rapidly growing new medium of human communication that encompasses text, graphics, video, and sound and is available instantly anywhere in the world.

Yahoo: Collection of Web- and Internet-based information categorized in a subject tree.

Résumé Skill Words List/ Sample Résumé

Use these lists to refine, expand, create, develop, improve, and design a more professional-looking résumé, but remember to be truthful in describing yourself and your various accomplishments. Consider describing yourself in terms of your skills rather than expecting potential employers to translate how your degrees and experience might be useful to them. Do not use a word you do not understand. Of course you are not limited to these lists. Resort to these lists after you have set your goals, identified your skills, selected your experience factors, and formulated the first draft of a résumé. Then use these lists or a thesaurus to amplify, clarify, develop, describe, and create the most attractive, eye-catching, and truthful résumé possible.

NOUNS

(Words used to name a person, place, object, idea, quality, or activity)

vendor	master_____	ability	wizard
_____smith	employee	facility	style
readiness	competence	dexterity	mode
technique	prowess	adroitness	expert
balance	energy	system	ease
deftness	posture	prospect	trend
status	communication	entrepreneur	poise
forecast	spontaneity	demeanor	vigor
bearing	high performer	appearance	mien
presence	manner	custom	look
praxis	practice	reputation	manager
prestige	station	stance	usage
attitude	agility	distinction	state
method	operative	composure	rank
résumé	work	capability	grace
exercise	pursuit	study	vitality
contact	habit	custom	urbanity
notoriety	message	report	rehearsal
supervisor	dignity	director	usage
official	foreperson	officer	character
pilot	administrator	leader	superintendent
altruism	guide	mentor	executive
honor	service	favor	chief
lookout	business	trade	conscience
firm	industry	commerce	kindness
outfit	corporation	establishment	company
occupation	vocation	job	enterprise
chore	effort	duty	employment
function	position	purpose	task
outlook	distinction	appointment	role
rectitude	uprightness	accolade	prospect
regard	appreciation	respect	integrity
worker	technician	esteem	respect
	expertise	craft	estimation

VERBS

(Words that express existence, action, or occurrence; in résumé writing you may find the past tense of these active verbs more accurate)

operate	supervise	compete	consider
encourage	able	balance	motivate
plan	affect	produce	organize
act	ease	conciliate	qualify
effect	energize	intellectualize	compose
facilitate	dignify	communicate	grace
settle	expedite	alleviate	handle
systematize	allay	evaluate	enunciate
forecast	market	deal	mitigate
assuage	characterize	entitle	function
customize	work out	pursue	trade
designate	exploit	implement	employ
exercise	beautify	embellish	actuate
use	admire	value	consider
enhance	distinguish	ennoble	esteem
regard	acclaim	extol	laud
elevate	conduct	oversee	fare
praise	purchase	administer	buy
govern	run	sequence	teach
educate	instruct	discipline	tutor
present	point	direct	aim
head	cast	level	zero in
correct	pass	follow up	trail
follow	sell	chase	rush
spark	appropriate	merchandise	vend
handle	evaluate	purchase	allocate
appoint	indicate	earmark	nominate
show	calculate	assess	denote
estimate	impose	specify	rate
assay	determine	judge	levy
review	conclude	exact	referee
gather	think	decide	infer
gauge	design	deduce	observe
develop	manage		

ADJECTIVES

(Words that answer the questions *what kind, how many,* or *which one;* the word modifies the meaning of a noun or pronoun)

skilled	serious	technical	effective
self-employed	energetic	earnest	proficient
businesslike	forceful	enterprising	no-nonsense
adept	strong	independent	peppy
vigorous	robust	powerful	ingenious
active	composed	calm	competent
qualified	productive	dexterous	instinctive
balanced	agile	graceful	political
expert	deft	conciliatory	handy
gentle	smart	alert	adroit
quick-witted	steady	intelligent	realistic
pragmatic	dynamic	high-performance	well-groomed
systematic	spontaneous	organized	quiet
dignified	artistic	practical	poised
artful	orderly	innovative	functional
methodical	uniform	tidy	complex
regular	constant	even	urbane
true	staunch	firm	stable
resolute	lively	steadfast	loyal
efficient	tasteful	driving	aesthetic
unprecedented	inventive	original	novel
bold	bright	creative	ingenious
keen	witty	sharp	sharp-witted
chic	modish	humorous	scintillating
wise	shrewd	stylish	dashing
perspicacious	amusing	frugal	astute
jocular	facetious	comical	zany
skillful	contingent	trim	shipshape
efficacious			

ADVERBS

(Words that answer the questions *when, where, why, in what manner,* or *to what extent*; the word modifies the meaning of a verb, an adjective, or another adverb; often ends in *-ly*)

effectively	efficaciously	astutely	seriously
earnestly	energetically	proficiently	actively
powerfully	vitally	forcefully	genuinely
surpassingly	robustly	quickly	tastefully
instinctively	gracefully	calmly	skillfully
easily	gently	expertly	deftly
realistically	pragmatically	quick-wittedly	efficiently
adroitly	smartly	steadily	quietly
distinctly	vigorously	systematically	neatly
quickly	dynamically	spontaneously	practically
expeditiously	briskly	effortlessly	masterly
functionally	attitudinally	cleverly	competently
orderly	ethnically	complexly	intelligently
dexterously	politically	independently	briskly
artistically	artfully	handily	accidentally
inadvertently	methodically	neatly	conditionally
smoothly	fortuitously	casually	fluidly
elegantly	fluently	relatively	tranquilly
coolly	exquisitely	imperturbably	nonchalantly
placidly	evenly	prettily	boldly
presumptuously	serenely	keenly	audaciously
brightly	impudently	knowingly	fashionably
wisely	alertly		

B.S., Education/1 Year Experience/Tutoring English Usage

Dona Frank   Voice: (656) 555-4326
3278 Main Street   Office: (656) 555-6754
Dayton, Michigan 00000   e-mail: Dfrank@000.edu

CAREER FOCUS   *Elementary Education/English Tutor/Reading Readiness,* where developed skills in English composition, reading comprehension, and child counseling will enable a school to improve its students' individual standings on national tests of reading and English usage; counseling the students with these deficiencies to improve their abilities within six to eight months.

SKILLS PROFILE

English Usage	*Reading*	*Counseling*
Sentence Structures	Vocabulary	Young Child
Grammar	Comprehension	Development
Usage Skills	Speed	Problem Solving
Story Building	Verbal Reading	Guidance
Spelling	Acting in Plays	Group Work

EDUCATION   **B.S. (Elementary Education)** University of Southern Michigan. Jackson, Michigan, cum laude

Significant Theory Courses:
Principles of Child Development
Education Theory (I, II, III)
English Composition

Important Lab Courses:
Speech Labs
Language Labs (English)
Lesson Planning Lab

Relevant Projects:
Practiced Teaching
Developed Training Tool for Slow Readers
Designed Spelling Lab for Computers (senior project)

EXPERIENCE   *Teaching Assistant.* St. Michael's Episcopal Elementary School. Jackson, Michigan (1999–2000)

Developed lesson plans under supervision of classroom teacher and presented these lessons to fifth graders for an eight-week student grading period.

Teaching Assistant. Inner-City Summer Curriculum. Jackson, Michigan (1999)

Volunteered for inner-city project to assist poor readers to improve their reading scores before going back to school in the fall. Results: 87 percent of students who attended the class improved their reading one to two grade levels as measured by national tests.

PROFILE SAMPLE

Dona Frank   Voice: (656) 555-4326
3278 Main Street   Office: (656) 555-6754
Dayton, Michigan 00000   e-mail: Dfrank@000.edu

POSITION

Elementary School Reading Specialist. Jackson County School District, #4, Moraine City, Michigan (1999–present)

SKILLS

(Wide variety of responsibilities within the district.)

Primary	Elementary	Administration
Vocabulary Drills	Reading Labs	Interdistrict Plans
Comprehension	Tests and Measures	Primary-Level View
Teacher Training	Comprehension	Gr. 4, 5, and 6 Designs

Other skills such as classroom management, teacher–student liaison, parent–teacher conferences, and individual student counseling occur at various times and situations within each month.

PROFESSIONAL ACCOMPLISHMENTS

Designed and implemented a new system for testing intermediate reading comprehension twice a year, resulting in better student performance on national tests.

Developed three grade levels within each primary division for more accurate measure of vocabulary skills, resulting in better comprehension and extended vocabulary among the three grade levels.

Designed a comprehensive teacher-training program for all teachers of primary students, resulting in early diagnosis of reading difficulties among students in grades 1, 2, and 3.

EDUCATION

M.A. (Elementary Reading Education) University of Michigan, Ann Arbor, Michigan

Current topics under study include psychology of reading, child physical and mental development, contemporary learning theories, and children's literature.

B.S. (Elementary Education) University of Southern Michigan. Jackson, Michigan, *cum laude*

Budget— 2000 Figures

Item	Description	Statistical Averages	Current Costs
Résumé preparation	Professional counseling	$175–$250/hour	
	Typesetting résumé	$100–$125/page	
	Word processing résumé	$25–$30/page	
	Reproducing résumé	$20/100 copies	
Letters	Stationery: ream of paper and 250 matching envelopes	$150	
	Typing letters and envelopes	$7–$10/letter	
	Postage	First class	
Telephone	Long-distance calls	As needed	
	Internet connections	$30/month	
	Local calls, pay phones	$0.50/3-minute call	
Transportation	Air travel	As needed	
	Ground travel: taxi, bus, tolls, parking, gas and oil	As needed	
Food	Restaurant expenses while job hunting	As needed	
Lodging	Hotel/motel expenses if needed for interviews	As needed	
Other	Newspapers/journals	As needed	
	Professional clothes	As needed	
	Meetings, seminars, courses	As needed	
Additional	Spouse or traveling companion(s)	As needed	

You and the Law

Historical Legal Considerations

THE CONSTITUTION OF THE UNITED STATES

Amendments 1 and 5 within the Bill of Rights forbid discrimination based on religion, guarantee free speech, and forbid deprivation of life, liberty, and the pursuit of happiness without due process of law.

CIVIL RIGHTS ACTS: 1886, 1871, 1964, 1968, 1972, 1974, 1986, 1987, 1991

In one way or another and sometimes in a summation of rights, the Constitution and its amendments guarantee freedom from discrimination based on religion, race, national origin, color, gender, age, physical or mental disabilities, and citizenship. These acts also require employers to provide accommodations for the disabled. Soon gender preference may also be covered under freedom from discrimination by others.

CONSTITUTIONAL PROTECTIONS. Davis-Bacon, Walsh-Healy, Wagner, Unemployment Compensation, Fair Labor Standards Act, Labor-Management Relations, Equal Pay, Occupational Safety and Health Administration (OSHA), Title VII Amendment, Equal Employment Opportunity Commission (EEOC), Vietnam-era Veteran's Readjustment, Privacy, Employee Retirement Income Security Act

(ERISA), Minimum Wage, Pregnancy Discrimination, 1980 Sexual Harassment Guidelines, Employee Polygraph Protection, Plant Closings, Family Medical Leave, and Gender Equity.

The listed legislative acts, among others on the books, provide various options for employees and in some cases employers. These collectively include guarantees of prevailing wages for government contractors, employees' right to organize, collective bargaining in management-labor disputes, and establishment of unions. In addition to these there are income for fired or laid-off employees, minimum wage, controlled hours, premium pay for overtime, control of hours children may work, good-faith bargaining in disputes, outlawing of closed shops, prohibition of strikes in national emergencies, equal pay for equal work, reasonably safe workplace, affirmative action, protection of employees' pension funds, diverse national workplace, pregnancy defined as a disability for benefits of disability coverage, freedom from sexual harassment, family medical leave, and gender equity.

What's Been Happening Lately?

See the following chart, which frames the ten top decisions of 1999 in employment law, as measured by the National Institute of Business Management in their newsletter *You and the Law: Quick and Easy Advice for Managing Employment Law Changes.* These decisions were made by a variety of judges using current employment laws. None is making history, but some will come up again and again. Ultimately someone in the House of Representatives will have to begin the process if one of these laws gets amended or if a new law is written about an old topic in employment circles.

TOP TEN CASES—EMPLOYMENT LAW

LAW	ISSUE	ADVICE	RULING
ADA	May employers consider mitigating measures (eyeglasses, medication) in determining ADA protection.	Treat every claim of ADA disability individually. Consider the effect of the mitigating measures when determining whether a major life activity is limited. Focus on ability with the mitigating measures, then focus on the ability to do the job.	Yes. #97-1943
FMLA	Several illnesses can be a "serious condition," even though not one of them would be considered so individually.	Err on the side of employee's claim of a serious health condition, but make sure you get medical documentation for each presumed illness.	Yes. CA 7 #96-2249
Title VII	Content of e-mail messages form the basis of a bias lawsuit and expose a company to Title VII liability.	E-mail's growing popularity and unmonitored use are putting employers at risk of being sued for employee discrimination. Employers could be held responsible for e-mail messages that demonstrate discriminatory practice or result in a hostile workplace.	Yes. USDC SDNY 96 Civ, 9747
EPA	Is performing comparable but not the same work enough reason for an employee to prevail under Equal Pay Act?	Employers cannot base an employee's wages on gender. The four basic factors the court considers are skill level, effort, responsibility, and working conditions.	No. CA 10 #96-3021
Title VII	Gender harassment that is not defined as sexual harassment can win a lawsuit claiming unlawful retaliation for that complaint.	Retaliation is the situation in this case. Employers are encouraged to keep clear, precise, and accurate records about an employee's performance, the facts, the people, and the employee's response. It is enough that the employee believed the conduct to be gender based and that her employer did not have solid documentation to support its true reasons for firing her.	Yes. NY S #95-10439
Title VII	Is a company put on notice if an employee makes a sexual harassment complaint to a department head?	Employers and employees need to review the company's sexual harassment policy to be sure it designates the persons and levels of responsibility for reporting the complaints. This should be in the procedure and policy guidelines.	Yes. CA 7 123F.3d672
FLSA	Are marketing reps considered "administrative employees" under the FLSA and exempt from overtime?	Owners are not relieved of their obligation to pay overtime merely by designating said employees as "marketing reps." The courts will examine closely an employee's duties, independence, and background to determine whether the exemption should be granted.	Yes. CA 1 #97-1053
Age	Can an employer eliminate a position because of automation without risking age discrimination liability?	Employers must prove business necessity. Restructuring a company must be done on a business necessity–only basis. That basis for decision must be communicated to all employees affected by the decision.	Yes. DDC #96-449

LAW	ISSUE	ADVICE	RULING
COBRA	Are general oral notifications of COBRA rights sufficient under the law?	COBRA requires that employers offer the opportunity for continued health coverage to former employees if a qualifying event, such as termination of employment, occurs.	No. CA 10 #96-5168
Title VII	Staff discrimination against interracial dating	Does Title VII prohibit discrimination based on an interracial relationship? Can an employer be held liable for discrimination by its supervisor, even if the employer was not aware of the discrimination?	Yes to both. 5th Cir #97-10685-CVOHTM, 1998

Index